What people are

The Magic of Cats

This is a wonderful book on the lore of cats. Andrew Anderson delves into their history, mythology, and folklore as well as studies into their behaviour, personalising his writing with delightful anecdotes about the feline companions with which he has shared his home. Cats have a two-sided reputation – sometimes worshipped as Gods, but at other times considered to be agents of the Devil. Seeing a cat can be a symbol of luck or an omen of misfortune. Anderson poetically describes these opposite views as 'The Cat of the Night and the Cat of the Day', exploring how these seemingly contradictory attributes add to the magic – and mystery – of cats.
Lucya Starza, author of Pagan Portals titles on *Candle Magic, Poppets and Magical Dolls, Guided Visualisations,* and *Scrying*

A charming, fascinating book full of insight into the furry mysteries who sometimes share our homes.
Nimue Brown, Druid and Author

The Magic of Cats is precisely that. It tells the story of our relationship with our feline friends, certainly, but also delves into the deeper mysticism, cosmic power and history of felis catus... making me look just a little harder at the small furry member of my own household. From one Cat to others, this book is a joy. Please do hunt it down.
Cat Treadwell, Pagan Priest and Author

The Magic of Cats is a fascinating look at how cats have been a part of magickal practice, folklore, and superstition for hundreds of years. Beautifully told through 'The Cat of the Night' and 'The

Cat of the Day', each section offers an insight into the power of our feline friends. A well-written and intriguing read into the world of cats, this is a great book for those who wish to understand why these creatures are considered so magical.

Jessica Howard, author of *The Art of Lithomancy*

This is a charming small tome for those with an interest in cats, magic or both. As a cat lover, I was instantly interested in reading this book and I imagine most cat lovers will enjoy this mixture of history, magic and general cat adulation.

Luke Eastwood, author of *The Druid Garden, The Druid's Primer* and *The Journey*

From Egyptian gods to witches' familiars, humans have always intuitively felt that cats are magical beings. Andrew Anderson's book, *The Magic of Cats*, joyfully traces our spiritual relationship with these enigmatic and wonderful creatures from an object of fear and worship to a beloved household companion that continues to fascinate and mystify animal lovers to this day.

Logan Albright, author of *Conform or Be Cast Out: The (Literal) Demonization of Nonconformists*

The Magic of Cats

The Magic of Cats

Andrew Anderson

MOON BOOKS

Winchester, UK
Washington, USA

JOHN HUNT PUBLISHING

First published by Moon Books, 2023
Moon Books is an imprint of John Hunt Publishing Ltd., No. 3 East Street, Alresford
Hampshire SO24 9EE, UK
office@jhpbooks.net
www.johnhuntpublishing.com
www.moon-books.net

For distributor details and how to order please visit the 'Ordering' section on our website.

ISBN: 978 1 80341 066 1
978 1 80341 067 8 (ebook)
Library of Congress Control Number: 2022938651

Illustrated by Hannah Willow

A CIP catalogue record for this book is available from the British Library.

Design: Matthew Greenfield

UK: Printed and bound by CPI Group (UK) Ltd, Croydon, CR0 4YY
Printed in North America by CPI GPS partners

We operate a distinctive and ethical publishing philosophy in
all areas of our business, from our global network of authors to
production and worldwide distribution.

Contents

For my boys, Marlowe and Alfie,
My Moon and Sun,
My Night and Day.

And to Whiskey, the first cat to show me
how wonderful felines could be.

Previous Titles by this Author

The Ritual of Writing
ISBN 978 1 78904 153 8

Artio and Artaois
ISBN 978 1 78904 462 1

Acknowledgements

Thank you to Hannah Willow for the stunning cover design and illustrations. I have been an admirer of Hannah's art for many years so to work with her on this project has been an honour and a delight. The spirit of her beloved George lives on in these wonderful illustrations.

Thank you to Trevor and all at Moon Books for their ongoing support and encouragement. It really is wonderful working with you.

Thank you to my sisters, Lesley and Jackie, who gifted me their love of cats. An extra-special thank you to Lesley for finding Alfie and bringing him home to me.

Thank you to Sue, for suggesting this book long before I had the opportunity to write it.

And, as always, to Becky for everything.

With happy memories and fondest thoughts of Nicky, Nicki, Topsy, Beebee, Jinx, Morris, Norman, Chip, Max, Jack, Dolly, Bert, Pickles, Eric, Tilly, Jake, Angus and the Ghost Cat

Introduction

There have always been cats in my life. When I was born, my family had a cat called Nicky. I have been told that, when I was learning to walk, I used to chase her around the house and try to catch her. No wonder my only memories are of her running away from me.

A short while after she died, we adopted a kitten that my brother's cat (another Nicki) had given birth to. I wanted the little male kitten named Whiskey but Mum and Dad didn't want a tom cat, so they took one of the female kittens and changed her name to Whiskey instead. Through most of my childhood, Whiskey had very little to do with me. There wasn't any animosity between us, it's just that I clearly belonged to our dog, Tina.

Tina died when I was 18 and, shortly after, Whiskey decided to inherit me as her human. She used to come and find me and hang out, as well as sleep on my bed at night. She really was the most gorgeous, gentle cat. She didn't seem to stray far from the back garden and I never once remember her bringing back any prey. When I went to University, Dad moved house. I was convinced that Whiskey would forget about me. However, on my first visit to the new place, Whiskey trotted down the garden path towards me and rolled onto her back to show me her tummy. It was almost as if she knew I was coming to visit.

When I moved in with my cat co-parent, Becky, we decided that we wanted a pet of our own. I wanted a puppy. What we got was a kitten and not just any kitten. We got the most wilful, single-minded being I have ever met. He was a little black and white bundle of energy and his name is Marlowe. From the moment I met him, I knew who was in charge. We were waiting in a friend's garden (which happened to be near a prison) and were going to collect the kitten from their neighbour. However, Marlowe had a different idea! He walked into my friend's garden, along with his mother and sister, as if he owned it. When I picked him up, he looked through me as if I wasn't there or simply wasn't important. Over the next few months, we learned that Marlowe got what Marlowe wanted. He was incredibly demanding, knocking things on the floor and trashing the furniture, to the point where I came home one day and found Becky pulling her hair out because Marlowe had trashed the Christmas tree AGAIN!

What, we wondered, if Marlowe had a friend, another cat with whom he could play, rather than demanding from us all of the time?

Shortly after, my sister asked if we could rehome a cat who had been dropped out of a high window in a block of flats. We agreed. The fellow who arrived was a big, lanky ginger tom called Alfie whose rough, tough exterior covered up a gentle and somewhat anxious heart. Happy to be beta to Marlowe's alpha, Alfie fitted right in and the pair were soon sleeping belly to belly on the couch. Life hasn't always stayed that peaceful but they are generally good mates.

Marlowe and Alfie are not our pets. They are our family and play as big a part in shaping our household as either of us humans. I refer to them as 'the boys'. However, that term has got me into trouble. I was talking about Marlowe and Alfie to a friend at work and was overheard by a nearby customer.

"Two boys?" she butted in. "How old are they?"

"They're both five," I replied.

"Twins, how wonderful!" she enthused.

"Oh, they're not twins" I said, bluntly. "One came from a prison and the other was thrown out of a window."

She needed a sit down and a glass of water while I explained they were cats.

One day, Becky said to me "we don't mythologize our boys enough". That night, as I was drifting off to sleep, I looked at Alfie and asked "How do I mythologize you? Do you have any myths of your own? How do you think the world was made?"

That question eventually led me to write a narrative poem for children called, "The Cat of the Night and the Cat of the Day", which put Marlowe and Alfie at the centre of a creation myth. In it, the Cat of the Night (who is black and white) and the Cat of the Day (who is ginger) chase each other around and around the Earth in an endless game. You can read the poem at the end of this book and find representations of these characters throughout and on the cover, illustrated by Hannah Willow.

The concept resonated so deeply with me that I turned the idea into two tattoos. On my left arm I have a paw print with the Moon and the Stars, on the right, a paw print with the Sun emerging from behind some clouds. Not only do the images evoke the idea of the left hand being intuitive and the right reflecting more conscious thought, but it also, coincidentally, reflects the sides where the cats prefer to sit. If they come for a cuddle Marlowe tends to sit on my left and Alfie on my right.

In the poem, the cats are purely the embodiment of night and day, but the more I thought about the concept of the Cat of the Night and the Cat of the Day, the more I saw within it. Within much common lore, it is generally accepted that the "cat is symbol of the night, of the lunar darkness and of the Moon's phases".[1] Through this symbolism, cats have gained a reputation for being spiritual, magical, somewhat other worldly creatures. While I think it is easy for us to recognize this representation of cats, it isn't something I could always see in the boys' behaviour. I became aware that they have another aspect, which is somewhat overlooked, but is just as magical. This aspect is grounded in the apparent world and the light of the sun. For many centuries, cats were associated with the sun, although the potency of that connection has faded and forgotten in recent centuries.

In writing this book, I hope to make the case that cats are beings of the day as much as they are of the night. I will use different iterations of the Cat of the Night (the Universal, Witch's and

Knowing Cats) and the Cat of the Day (the Idiomatic, Physical and Evolving Cats) to explore the two sides of these wonderful, intelligent and complex beings, with whom we share our lives.

The Cat of the Night

Who is the Cat of the Night?

The Cat of the Night by Hannah Willow

So, the Cat of the Night with the black, black nose,
With the Moon on his chest and stars on his toes,
Was a gift to the Earth, as a sign of great love
From her Silvery Mother in the dark sky above.

In my poem, the Cat of the Night is the embodiment of night time and darkness, who rolls out of the skirts of the Moon. As he runs around the Earth, he brings darkness with him; the cool of a summer's evening and the chill of a deep winter's night. He ushers in not only the night-time but the dark half of the year, when "night times are long and day times are short". The Moon, ever protective of her creation, watches from the sky as the shadow of the Cat of the Night passes over the Earth.

The Moon casts her silvery light on the chest of the Cat of the Night, turning his black fur purest white. Primarily, this was done so that the kitten would more closely resemble my cat, Marlowe. However, there is a deeper, subconscious point being made here as the Moon brands the Cat as a creature of her own. The connection between cats and the Moon is long established in both magical and common lore, inspiring myth and poetry across the centuries. It is the cat's eye, particularly its pupil, which can change from a thin, vertical line to full and round, which many have felt echoes the waxing and waning of the Moon.

Through that connection, the cat became a creature that is seen as both magical and changeable. Anyone who lives with a cat knows this to be the case. Marlowe is a particularly changeable cat. He can go from affectionate to aloof or, even worse, annoyed in the blink of an eye. While this sense of being changeable is now a source of gossip and amusement between cat lovers, it hasn't always seemed such a benign quality. With the idea that cats are changeable came the inference that they are somehow dishonest, scheming, even malicious. To be fair, I can see where that assumption comes from. Sometimes, when I look Marlowe in the eye, I just know he is plotting to take over the world. There is an intelligence about him, and about many cats, that makes their owners question who really has the control in their relationship. Thankfully, for me, the answer is clear. Marlowe is in charge.

Through their association with the Moon, cats have also become closely associated with a number of different goddesses. While some goddesses have manifested as cats, or had feline elements to their physiology, others have cats who are associated or work with them. This has given the cat a strong feminine energy, which we still see manifested around us; for example, we often find cats referred to using the feminine pronoun. Marlowe is an exceptionally pretty cat; he has a small build and very delicate features. The number of times people have assumed he is a she is, I am sure, a source of great annoyance to him. It's worth me saying at this stage that the Cat of the Night appears as a male cat in the poem solely because he is based on Marlowe, who would be very annoyed if I changed it.

Alongside their association with the Moon, cats are frequently connected with aspects of darkness. This probably comes from the idea that cats hunt at night, going off to search for prey while their humans stay indoors next to a warm fire (or television set). Cats actually prefer hunting at liminal times of half-light, such as dusk and dawn, but the association between cats and the night time is an enduring one. Although neither of my cats go out very often, if Marlowe wants to go out, it is generally at night. When I let him out into the darkness, he will very often just sit in the middle of the back yard, his coat concealing him within the shadows, as if he is somehow drinking in the very night itself. I have often asked him "Are you enjoying yourself out there, in the darkness?" to which I imagine him replying, "I'm not *in* the darkness. I *am* the darkness!"

The association of cats with both darkness and being malicious led their species into real danger with superstitious humans. The idea of the cat skulking off into the night for a secret, 'other' life has given them a somewhat shadowy reputation, connecting them to the dark arts and positioning them as the familiars of witches. Add to this their inherent sense of intelligence and we can perhaps see why many were thought not to be animals at all, but disguised incarnations of devils and demons. For centuries, cats were persecuted and tortured because of these beliefs, innocent casualties of the darkest side of human nature.

Having exposed the darker side of humanity, it is somewhat appropriate that cats seem able to peer into the murkiest recesses of the human psyche. They make a perfect guide to the human subconscious. I have already mentioned the day that we collected Marlowe for the first time and how he looked through me as if I wasn't there. I often get the sense that he is assessing me or evaluating me, often knowing how I feel before I do. In fact, there are many recorded accounts of cats seeming to behave in pre-emptive or psychic ways – and we may have experienced one with Marlowe. For years we felt terrible about the way that we just picked him up and took him away from his mother and sister when they happened to walk through the garden where we were waiting. Then, one day it occurred to me that maybe, just maybe, it wasn't a coincidence that Marlowe's mother happened to be there with her kittens. Rather than simply having taken him out for a walk, what if she came to meet us, to entrust her little boy to us? I can't prove it, but the coincidence of her walking through that space where two unknown humans were waiting seems very strange.

It also begs the question that if cats can 'see through' us and even predict the future, what else can they see? There is a long tradition that cats can see ghosts and spirits. This may well be a superstition which arises from the association of cats with witches, but every cat lover will tell you about a time when their cat stared intently at an empty space for no apparent reason. "What are you looking at?" we ask when they do that, although we barely ever get a reply.

It's not just the case that cats may be able to see ghosts but also that people often report seeing cats that are ghosts. Again, this is something I have experienced. When I came to look around my current home, I was convinced I saw a feline walk through one of the rooms, although the previous owner told me they did not have a cat. Since living here, I have occasionally seen, out of the corner of my eye, a cat walk into the room. I have greeted Marlowe or Alfie warmly, only to find out that they are somewhere else and fast asleep. I have often commented that, when one of the boys starts running around the house, that it's likely they are being chased by the ghost cat.

However, it is not the Moon nor the darkness of this world, the human psyche nor the otherworld, which will provide our starting point in this section of the book. We will begin with the stars. The inspiration, as always, came from Marlowe himself. As he has got older, Marlowe's "black, black" fur has become flecked with grey and white hairs. Little constellations have appeared on the midnight of his coat. The Cat of the Night is becoming the Cat of the Cosmos. It made me muse that looking up at the stars takes us on a journey back through time to the beginning of all things. That simple act of looking upwards leads us away from earthly concerns and out, towards the universal.

And that is the perfect place to begin our journey to explore the deep magic of the archetypal otherworldly cat of myth and legend, the seer in the darkness and stalker of shadows – the Cat of the Night.

Chapter 1

The Cat of the Night – The Universal Cat

The Universal Cat by Hannah Willow

Did you know that there was, for a very short time, a constellation known as *Felis* or *The Cat*? It was proposed by astronomer and all-round cat lover Joseph Jérôme Lalande in 1799 and actually made it onto some star charts in the early 1800s, placed between the constellations of Hydra and Antilla:

> Some authorities say that he did this to spite Voltaire, distinctly not a cat-lover, who had argued that the cat did not know how to achieve a place among the constellations where such other animals as bears, dogs, lions, bulls and the like were secure ... 'I am very fond of cats,' [Lalande] wrote. 'I will let this figure scratch on the chart. The starry sky has worried me quite enough in my life, so that now I can have my joke with it.[1]

Well, as any cat owner knows, you can't tell a cat to stay in one place and, shortly after, the cat constellation disappeared, written out of the star charts. The story doesn't end there, though, and the cat has been recently been put back into our night sky. In June 2018, star number HR3923 within the Hydra constellation, was called *Felis* in honour of Lalande's work.

Despite this relatively recent move to secure the cat's place in the cosmos, the association between cats and stars goes back much further. Stories tell us of the great Persian Holy Warrior, Rustam, and his many trials and adventures. In one tale in particular, Rustam discovered an old man being attacked by a band of thieves. He immediately drew his sword and fought off the bandits, before taking the gentleman to a safe distance. There he lit a campfire to keep the old man warm. As night fell and the chill desert breeze stoked the flames of the fire, the old man asked Rustam how he could reward him as a thank you for saving his life. Ever modest, Rustam refused to take anything. "I have the warmth of the fire, the smell of the smoke and the light of the stars high above me. What else do I need?" Rustam replied.

It was then that the old gentleman revealed his true nature. He was not a defenceless old man but a magician and a very powerful magician, too. He stretched out one hand and grasped a fistful of smoke which billowed from the campfire. With his other hand he reached into the fire itself and took hold of some of the flames. Bringing his hands together he began forming a small, intricate magical object. The magician then reached up into the indigo sky, picked two of the brightest stars and added them into the mixture. When he had finished, the magician opened his hands and was holding a tiny, smoky grey kitten with eyes as bright and brilliant as the stars overhead. And that is how the Persian cat came to be created, as a gift to Rustam, and the world, after an act of great bravery.

A similar tale, of how the act of one person created a whole breed of cats, can be found relating to the tabby cat. The Prophet

Muhammed (PBUH) was a great lover of cats and had a feline companion called Muezza. We shall hear more about them later in this book, but it was Muhammed's love for Muezza which led to the letter M appearing in stripes on the foreheads of all tabbies.

For me, this wonderful tale has resonances of William Blake's poem *The Tyger*:

Tyger Tyger, burning bright,
In the forests of the night:
What immortal hand or eye,
Could frame thy fearful symmetry?

In what distant deeps or skies
Burnt the fire of thine eyes!
On what wings dare he aspire?
What the hand, dare seize the fire?

And what shoulder, & what art,
Could twist the sinews of thy heart?
And when thy heart began to beat,
What dread hand? & what dread feet?

What the hammer? what the chain,
In what furnace was thy brain?
What the anvil? what dread grasp,
Dare its deadly terrors clasp?

When the stars threw down their spears
And water'd heaven with their tears:
Did he smile his work to see?
Did he who made the Lamb make thee?

Tyger, Tyger burning bright,
In the forests of the night:

What immortal hand or eye,
Dare frame thy fearful symmetry?[2]

The "fearful symmetry" of Blake's Tyger has always reminded me of the patterning of a tabby cat, the smaller 'Tyger' who stalks our homes. We also get an echo of Rustam's tale, as the Tyger's eyes burn like stars from "distant deeps and skies", but here it is the Judeo-Christian God who creates the creature, rather than a magician. Blake uses imagery of the industrial revolution, showing the Tyger forged in the furnace of the universe like a beautiful machine. It is the contrast between the pure industrial strength and the artistry of the cat, along with the awesome strength of the creator, which makes the poem so compelling.

So far, we have considered stories which explore how cats were created, although there is a particularly wonderful Chinese myth, of how cats were involved in the creation of the Earth itself. The story goes that when the gods created the Universe, they decided that the most beautiful part of their creation, the Earth, needed special protection and monitoring. They considered which of all the species they created would be the most effective protectors of the wonderful planet and eventually settled upon cats. The gods imbued cats with the power of speech, so that they could report their findings, before leaving the planet in the capable paws of its new overseers.

However, when the gods returned to Earth, they found the cats had been very negligent in their duties. They preferred to lay in the shade of trees or chase insects, rather than looking after the planet. The gods gave cats a good talking to and left them clear instructions before leaving them to get on with the job once again. A second divine inspection of the planet revealed that, once again, the cats hadn't followed the gods' instructions at all and were still not looking after it properly. They preferred to doze in the sunshine and groom their beautiful coats, rather than keep an eye on what was going on around them. Once again, the gods told cats very clearly what they expected of them before leaving them in charge once more.

The gods came back for a third time but, instead of finding any improvement in their behaviour, they found the cats were still lounging around, chasing leaves and blossom petals and really not doing their job at all. When the gods asked why the why they weren't doing as they were asked, the cats explained that they really had far better things to be doing than running the world which, frankly, seemed a bit beneath them. The gods were in disarray – what were they going to do now? Who was going to look after their planet? The cats suggested that humans seemed to be fairly decent types and maybe they should have a go at looking after the Earth instead. The gods agreed, removing the power of speech from cats and giving it to humans instead. However, the gods soon found out that humans were a pretty useless bunch and so cats were asked to stick close by and keep an eye on what humans were up to. And that is why cats live with us but often seem to be superior to us; we may have the power of speech but they are the ones who really run the world!

Through these stories we get a sense of cats having associations with the stars and the Earth, but their primary association is with the Moon. As Anna Franklin wrote: "To the ancients the cat seemed to be an animal of the moon, its changing eyes reflecting its waxing and waning".[3] Fred Gettings takes this idea one stage further, exploring the connection of the cat and the Moon in modern occult practice:

> The cat thrives in the darkness for it is an occult creature, happier in the reflected light of the Moon than the bright glare of the Sun's rays. The Sun in the sky is too steady for the everlasting cat, for her strange eyes are designed to fluctuate from full to slit, in imitation of that lesser luminary, the Moon. The cat is symbol of the night, of the lunar darkness and of the Moon's phases.[4]

For me, this connection finds its clearest expression in W.B. Yeats' beautiful and vibrant poem *The Cat and the Moon*:

> The cat went here and there
> And the moon spun round like a top,
> And the nearest kin of the moon
> The creeping cat, looked up...
> Does Minnaloushe know that his pupils
> Will pass from change to change,
> And that from round to crescent,
> From crescent to round they range?[5]

The connection between cat and the Moon is presented in the poem as instinctual and symbiotic. Yeats goes beyond simply presenting the cat as affected by the Moon, instead suggesting that his Universal Cat, Minnaloushe, can affect the Moon as well:

> Maybe the moon may learn,
> Tired of that courtly fashion,
> A new dance turn.[6]

Here we see that the Universal Cat is a potent symbol of change in and of itself, rather than simply a channel for the energy of the Moon.

The relationship between the cat and the Moon may have begun with the pupil of the cat's eyes but has not been limited to that single feature. For example, "Pliny said that a she cat would bear a total of twenty-eight kittens during her lifetime – the same number as the days in a lunar cycle".[7] We even find a parallel in Lewis Carroll's novel *Alice's Adventures in Wonderland* where the Cheshire Cat "vanished quite slowly, beginning at the end of the tail, and ending with a grin, which remained sometime after the rest of it had gone"[8], the smile being reminiscent of the Moon's crescent phase. This broader set of connections illustrate how the cat and the Moon, throughout history, have indeed been "kin", just as Yeats suggests.

With its connection to the Moon, the cat also gained associations and "magical attributes" which "are lunar and feminine in their vibration, with the qualities of the maternal nurturing mother and protector of her family".[9] While I don't, personally, agree with all of this statement and find it somewhat reductive, the association between the Moon and the feminine principle is, in itself, an interesting one.

Dr Charles Muses, an American philosopher and author, suggested that in many earlier religions all over the world the Moon deities tended to be males, while the Sun deities tended to be female; then somewhere along the line the male and female roles appeared to reverse. According to Charles Muses, the earlier female priests (or priestesses) honoured he Sun goddesses. But when the male priests took over they decided that as the sun provided more light (and therefore more power), it must be male; and so the female label was often given to the Moon of lesser light.[10]

Assuming Muses' suggestion is correct, this provides and interesting insight into the gender of deities who are associated with cats. In term of gods, there are very few who have connections with cats of any kind. The most notable of these is Ra, the Egyptian god of the Sun, who I will consider, briefly, later in this book. However, in a diversity of cultures around the world, we find many goddesses who have strongly and abiding associations with felines.

Perhaps the most notable of these is one of Egypt's most ancient deities. The daughter of Ra and Isis, Bastet, also known as Bast, was, originally, a lion headed goddess worshipped in the city of Bubastis. Over time, Bastet's reputation spread and her form changed, with her lion aspect changing into the head of a domesticated cat. As such, all cats became seen as an incarnation of the goddess and were therefore both worshipped and subject to strict ritualistic and legal requirements. "It was illegal to export them, and anyone who killed a cat was put to death".[11] Families whose cats died went into a period of mourning and had to shave off their eyebrows as a sign of their grief. The bodies of many adored family pets were taken to Bastet's temple in Bubastis where they were mummified.

In what he calls a "sad contrast to the ancient worship of the cat", Desmond Morris recounted what happened to many of these mummified bodies when the British occupied Egypt: "a consignment of 300,000 mummified cats were shipped to Liverpool where they were ground up and used as fertilizer on the fields of local farmers. All that survives from this episode is a single cat skull which is now in the British Museum".[12] I think it's fair to say that Bastet would not have been happy with the ultimate fate of her precious felines and neither were many cat lovers. This is merely one example of disregard and cruelty with which humanity has treated cats over the centuries. This book will, unfortunately, contain many more.

In terms of her role, clues to Bastet's characteristics can be found in her written name. Her hieroglyph has been recorded as "a perfume jar"[13], but is more probably an "ointment jar"[14] connecting her to a role of healing. She also had associations which arose from "Egyptian's observations of cats' natural abilities" and thus became connected to "family, joy, dance, music, sexuality, motherhood and fertility".[15] She was also considered a strongly protective goddess, not only for pregnant women (who would carry a talisman of Bastet with them) but of her own father:

It was believed that every day she would ride through the sky with her father, the sun god Ra. As his boat pulled the sun through the sky she would watch over and protect him.

At night, she would turn into a cat to protect Ra from his greatest enemy, the serpent Apep.[16]

I particularly like this story as we find that connection between cats (or a cat-headed goddess) and their protective role over their family at night. For many in the ancient world, cats would have had that role anyway, helping to protect the family's grain from mice and other creatures who sought an easy meal.

Bastet was loved and revered, but there was another cat goddess in Egypt who engendered a totally different reaction. She was the yin to Bastet's yang, the night to Bastet's day. She is also considered by many to be Bastet's sister. Sekhmet was the goddess of plague, "war, famine and destruction"[17] and was created by Ra to punish humanity after they failed to follow his rules. In one particularly nihilistic story, Sekhmet "kills and drinks the blood of humanity, retiring in the evening only to start again the next day. She does not stop and threatens to destroy humanity all together. The gods became concerned and flooded the land with beer, stained with pomegranate juice. Next morning Sekhmet ready and hungry for more killing sees the red liquid and thinking it to be blood begins to drink. She gets so drunk, completely forgets what she is doing and returns home. Humanity is saved from ultimate destruction".[18]

Just in case the gods weren't able to subdue Sekhmet with alcohol, Egyptians had a number of spells and rituals which could be used to protect themselves from her fearsome power. They would "whisper their prayers into the ears of cat mummies".[19] This clearly illustrates the difference between Sekhmet and Bastet in the Egyptian psyche: while the living cat was the embodiment of Bastet, in death it became a portal to communicate with the unsettling forces of Sekhmet. However, the Egyptians also found that they could call on Sekhmet for help in a tight spot. "Pharoah would take the spirit of Sekhmet into battle to be sure of victory against the enemies of Egypt".[20] Sekhmet was also considered to be a powerful and potent goddess of healing. Whatever the nature of your physical complaint, whatever force, deity or trickster had unleashed it upon you, Sekhmet could be counted on to bring equal force and vigour in your healing.

The duality that we find in Bastet and Sekhmet can also be found in Judaeo-Christianity, where cats represent both virginal and fallen, even demonic, women. With their reputation for being independent and having become a symbol of "lust and fecundity",[21] it is little surprise to find that cats have become associated with the figure of Adam's first wife. Lillith is a figure from Jewish folklore who has acquired some demonic associations. However, she is also believed to be the first woman, created from earth, like Adam. Refusing to accept Adam's rule over her, she left the garden of Eden. In some versions of the story, on her exit, "Lillith became a black cat".[22]

There is also a connection between cats and Jesus' mother, Mary. This is surprising, considering that cats were seen as highly sexual creatures. However, in a popular and really very charming story, at the same time as Mary was giving birth to Jesus, a cat was delivering her litter of kittens in the same stable. The connection between these two deliveries is a surprising one:

> ...there was also a belief in the antique world that the cat was impregnated by the ear. This notion is relevant to the 'Virgin cat' story, because it was widely believed that the Virgin Mary conceived Jesus through her ear, whilst listening to the Holy Spirit. Almost certainly the symbolism behind this curious belief is rooted in the idea of Christ as the Logos, the Word, issuing as it were from the mouth of God.[23]

The Welsh goddess, Ceridwen, is believed to work with cats in a similar way, using them to manifest thoughts and words into action. In some versions of the story where Ceridwen creates a potion to help her son, Afagddu, she is accompanied in her efforts by two white cats. They carry out her orders, collecting ingredients and returning them to her, so that the potion can be brewed. Little more is said about these two cats, although it is worth noting that they find parallels in the figures of Morda and Gwion Bach (who ultimately becomes the poet Taliesin) who stir Ceridwen's cauldron and tend the fire.

Another goddess who works with a team of felines is the Norse Goddess Freyja who rides a chariot drawn by cats (anyone who has ever tried to get two or more Cats to move in the same direction will understand just how skilled Freyja must have been to get them to pull a chariot). However, the reason why cats are associated with Freyja is somewhat mysterious. It could be another example of their association with lust and sexuality, as we saw with Lillith. Kevin Crossley-Holland writes that "Freyja was invoked by Pre-Christian Scandinavians as goddess of love, and is portrayed in the myths as sexually attractive and free with her favours".[24] However, there could be another reason for the association between cats and Freyja which suggest a more magical partnership. H.R. Ellis Davidson links Freyja to the vǫlva, a type of shaman or witch, suggesting that Freyja was the first to teach them magic:

> The use of animal fur in the costume of the *vǫlva* links up with the statement made by Snorri that Freyja travelled in a carriage drawn by cats. The link between cats and the goddess has not been satisfactorily explained, but the gloves made of cat skin, white and furry inside, mentioned in the Greenland account, suggest that cats were among the animal spirits which would aid the *vǫlva* on her supernatural journey.[25]

With both Ceridwen and her cauldron and Freyja's link to the vǫlva, we are beginning to move away from the realm of the Universal Cat and coming closer to a connection which has seen cats both celebrated and persecuted over many centuries. We are beginning to step into the realm of the Witch's Cat where cats became less revered and more feared, branded as imps and familiars. To make that connection we need to consider the cat's association with another goddess: Hekate.

Chapter 2

The Cat of the Night – The Witch's Cat

The Witch's Cat by Hannah Willow

Many Greek myths begin with an indiscretion being undertaken by a male and end up with a female being punished. The one I am about to tell you is no different. This is the story of how Zeus, king of the gods, disguised himself as the Theban general Amphitryon to seduce Amphitryon's wife, Princess Alcmene. Amphitryon had been fighting a war far from home, so Zeus took his form and told Alcmene that he had returned from the battle early. After an afternoon of passion, Alcmene conceived a child, who would grow up to be Heracles.

As an interesting feline aside, Amphitryon returned home later the same day and Alcmene conceived a child by him too. This is an example of superfecundation, where a female can become pregnant by two different males at the same time. This is common in cats, where a single litter of kittens can have two (or more) fathers.

On finding out that Alcmene was pregnant with Zeus' child, his wife, Hera was furious. She sent her daughter, the goddess of childbirth, Eileithyia, to sit outside of Alcmene's bedroom and cast a spell so that the child could not be born at the appointed time. This would mean it would have a different astrological birth chart and, therefore, a different destiny. Eileithyia immediately sat on the floor outside of Alcmene's room and wove her magic.

However, in forming their plan, neither Hera nor Eileithyia had considered Alcmene's clever and somewhat cunning servant, Galinthias (everyone *always* overlooks the servants, don't they?). Galinthias was aware that some sort of meddling magic was going on outside of the bedroom and so, in an attempt to stop it, announced that the baby had been born. Eileithyia was so stunned by the announcement that she stopped casting her spell and so, just at the appointed astrological moment, Alcmene gave birth to her son, Heracles.

Hera's hatred of Heracles is well documented, but she also took a bitter revenge on Galinthias for foiling her plan. As a punishment for her cunning, Galinthias was turned into a cat and sent to live in the Underworld with the Greek goddess of the Moon, magic and witchcraft, Hekate.

Cats were closely associated with Hekate and the reason comes from an earlier myth, one which involved the terrifying giant called Typhon. Typhon was simply enormous, so big that his head, which writhed with snakes, use to knock the stars from their orbit. While he had the body of a man, from the legs down he was coiled and scaly like a snake. During a particularly nasty encounter with Typhon, Hekate took the form of a cat in order to escape with her life. As a way of thanking cats for their assistance, Hekate bestowed a special blessing upon all felines and they became sacred to her.

Hekate's role as goddess of witchcraft has spread far beyond ancient Greece. While many modern practitioners work with her, we only have to look at earlier texts to find that the association between cats and Hekate was not always a positive one. Take, for example, Hekate's presentation in Shakespeare's play *Macbeth*, where she upbraids the three witches for not involving her in their meddlesome plot. When asked why she looks angry, Hekate replies:

> And I, the mistress of your charms,
> The close contriver of all harms,
> Was never called to bear my part
> Or show the glory of our art? (3.5.6-9)

The character is angry that she wasn't able to lead the witches in their destruction of the protagonist, portraying her as malicious and cruel. Later in this scene, created to feed the audience's desire to see such spectacle (believed by many to be an addition by Thomas Middleton, a contemporary of Shakespeare), Hekate cavorts with a number of spirits, notably, one in the shape of a cat. When Hekate asks the cat spirit, "What news?", it reveals itself to be as meddlesome as its mistress, revelling in disruption and stating, "All goes still to our delight" (3.5.53).

And so, through their association with Hekate, cats, which had once been the physical embodiment of a goddess on Earth, "the revered, sacred feline of ancient Egypt became the wicked, sorcerer's cat of medieval Europe".[1] However, this association went far beyond human practitioners of magic to their shadowy, all-powerful master.

> Because they had been involved in earlier pagan rituals, cats were proclaimed evil creatures, the agents of Satan ... Christians everywhere were urged to inflict as much pain and suffering on them as possible. The sacred had become the damned.[2]

Of course, this association between cats and witchcraft has had an enduring influence on our collective psyche and still finds expression in popular culture, particularly in entertainment aimed at young people. I first remember finding this connection in Helen Nicoll and Jan Pieńkowski's *Meg and Mog* books, which I loved as a child. The character of Zachary Binx is turned into a talking feline by the Sanderson Sisters in Disney's 1993 movie *Hocus Pocus* while, in the TV series *Sabrina the Teenage Witch*, the titular character has a witty black cat named Salem. Interestingly, it is the single female protagonist, Hermione Granger, who is the only central character to have a cat companion in the *Harry Potter* series of books. While many of these presentations seem to soften or ameliorate the connection between cats and witches, there are still some problematic presentations of felines in children's literature.

Take, for example, Ursula Moray William's 1942 (but still in print) novel *Gobbolino the Witch's Cat*. In the story, Gobbolino, who is born to a witch's familiar, Grimalkin, desperately tries to shake off his role as a witch's cat. What he really wants is to be a kitchen cat and "sit by the fire with my paws tucked under my chest and sing like the kettle on the hob".[3] Towards the end of the novel, after many adventures and rejections, Gobbolino is completely exasperated by the role life has given him: "I never wanted to be a witch's cat – not I! Witches are cruel and wicked and bad! They do evil and make people miserable! They come to a bad end, and nobody is sorry! They are bad! Bad! BAD!!".[4]

Another group of obviously manipulative witch's cats can be found in John Masefield's 1927 (but, again, still in print) children's novel *The Midnight Folk*. Protagonist Kay Harker is surrounded by a number of different cats throughout this story, including the resourceful, amiable Nibbins, but it is arch witch Sylvia Daisy Pouncer's sly, tricksy cats, with somewhat familiar names, who take active part in ritualistic magic: "Blackmalkin appeared, bearing a red light. After him came Mrs. Pouncer, crowned and wearing a long robe covered in magical signs; she bore a staff or wand. After her came Greymalkin, bearing a smoking dish".[5] At the end of the novel, both Greymalkin and Blackmalkin are apparently reformed, although they have been so underhand all the way through, the reader cannot be sure that this is really the case.

One thing to note in both texts is the name Greymalkin or Grimalkin. It is also heard in *Macbeth*, where the initial meeting of the three witches seems to be broken up by the meowing of a cat. The First Witch suddenly breaks the flow of conversation to reply "I come Grimalkin" (1.1.8). The name has an interesting history. Martha Gray suggests that "The name 'Grimalkyn' is derived from grim or *greom*, a word for the colour grey, and 'Malkin' being a version of the name Maud or Matilda meaning 'cat'.[6] Gettings takes the derivation of the name one step further, suggesting that the name Malkin:

>...was often given to the pagan Queen of the May, who had overtones of the 'old religion' or witchcraft in her bones ... The Matilda or Malkin name [became] changed to 'Marian', for the May-lady is the village girl who is crowned Queen of the May. The name has become that of Maid Marion, Robin Hood's lover...[7]

With such strong pagan overtones, it is little wonder that, in fanatical Christian times, the name "was associated with an old female cat that was ill tempered and aggressive".[8]

Grimalkin isn't the only cat's name that has survived the centuries. We know from the records of witch trials that cats variously named Sathan, Rutterkin, Holt, Bess and Pyewackett were accused of either aiding or leading accused witches in their evil actions. The reason these names were recorded is particularly interesting: "It was believed that the cat was merely a disguise for a demon, and if the name of the demon was known, it would be possible to exorcise it more easily".[9] We only have to think back to the idea that both the Virgin Mary and cats were impregnated through their ears, as presented in the last chapter, to see how words, or in this case names, were believed to have real power.

So, how did a witch come to work with such a powerful creature? Well, the process took the form of a ritual, which can be seen in many woodcuts of the time, in often surprisingly graphic detail. There stands the Devil, all black and shaggy, with a cheeky grin on his face, sticking his bottom out. Behind him, on her knees, is the witch, puckering her lips and going in to plant a kiss on the Devil's behind. Yes, it really was, apparently, as unpleasant as that. In return for literally 'kissing ass', witches were given an imp, or familiar, small demons which appeared in the shape of animals. Often, these familiars would appear in the form of a cat. This led to the belief that one should never beat nor drown a cat, or the Devil himself would come after you. Unfortunately, for felines, this didn't protect them for long and many cats found themselves being persecuted just for being cats.

Once a witch had made their pact with the Devil and secured their familiar, a physical change would happen to their body. The witch would need to suckle or feed their familiar with their own blood, meaning that they essentially needed another nipple from which the familiar could drink. This became known as the witch's teat or mark, which would be searched for during witch trials. These marks were often no more than moles or warts, but, to the frenzied witch hunters, they became a sure sign of a pact with the Devil.

Once a witch had sealed their pact with Satan and suckled their familiar, the Imp would begin working for them. In many accounts from witch trials, it appears that it is the cat rather than the human who is in control of events. Quite often the familiars were accused of killing either people or animals, sometimes whole herds of cattle. In fact, the accusations became so potent that simply having a cat became enough evidence that you were a witch. For example, "in an Exeter trial an old woman was condemned to be hanged because a neighbour testified that she had seen a cat jump into the window of her cottage one evening, and had believed it to be the Devil".[10]

Further, it wasn't just that people felt that cats were demons or imps, they sometimes believed that cats were people. "The most infamous witch trial judge of the sixteenth century, Jean Bodin, [insisted] that all cats are witches in disguise".[11] There are several reports of cats running away from the scene of an inexplicable event towards the house of a suspected witch. When followed, the cat was nowhere to be found but the witch would be there, with some evidence implicating that she had been at the scene. For example, a report of witchcraft from Thurso involved a merchant being plagued by cats. He killed two of them and chopped the leg off another. "Shortly afterwards a suspect called Helen Andrew died suddenly, and at the same time another was drowned. A third old woman, Margaret Nin-Gilbert, was seen to have a leg missing".[12]

There were several types of cats that were particularly suspicious and likely to be involved in such malevolent activities. The first of these is a brindled cat, which, again can be found in association with the Witches in *Macbeth*. "Thrice the brindled cat hath mewed" (4.1.1) the First Witch says at the start of the scene, as if the cat is prompting them to stand around the cauldron to begin making their magic potion. The word 'brindled' means "brown or grey streaked or patched with a darker colour"[13] and derives from the word 'branded'. As such, there is some difference of opinion over exactly what a brindled cat looks like. Some suggest brindled cats are tabby cats, which do indeed look as though their coat has been 'branded'. However, there doesn't seem to be very much folklore or superstition to back this up. In fact, in *Gobbolino the Witch's Cat*, when the titular character is found to have "a faint sheen of tabby",[14] it is a sign that he isn't really suited to life as a witch's cat. As Moray Williams uses other folkloric elements in her novel, this would be a strange omission. Others suggest that a brindled cat is actually "a female tortoiseshell cat".[15] There is more magical lore around tortoiseshell cats. The English considered them to be unlucky at one stage, so it is possible that these were the original brindled cats. However, whether tabby or tortoiseshell, brindled cats were not as suspicious as black cats.

The connection between black cats and witchcraft goes back centuries, beginning with their association with Hekate who "Although more often associated with black hounds" is often "depicted along with black cats".[16] As I have already mentioned, in Medieval times the Devil was often presented as being black and furry, so the fact that black coated animals were seen as aligned with evil is not really surprising. The connection between black cats and witches is so ingrained in western culture that it has left behind an incredible amount of folklore and superstition. According to Herbie Brennan, "A black cat crossing your path is a herald of good luck. But beware if crossing a black cat's path for then the luck will be bad".[17] There is a significant amount of regional variation in these beliefs:

> "...in Ireland a black cat walking across your path by moonlight meant a death in an epidemic ... In Yorkshire owning a black cat is supposed to be lucky while meeting one by accident on your path is not. If the cat was to walk towards you then it would bring good fortune, but if it walked away then it would take good fortune with it".[18]

Whether black cats are inherently lucky or unlucky for humans, their association with witches was nothing but bad luck for them.

In fact, the association between witches and black cats has actually shaped the genetics of the black cats alive today. In his seminal book *Catwatching*, zoologist Desmond Morris asks the question, "Why do so many black cats have a few white hairs?".[19] The answer is heartbreaking.

> The Christian Church organized burning-cats-alive ceremonies on the day of the Feat of Saint John. For these cruel rituals the most wicked and depraved of 'Satan's felines' were strongly preferred and all-black cats were eagerly sought out for the flames. But these cats had to be totally black to be really evil, in the minds of the pious worshippers. Any touch of white on their black coats might be taken as a sign that they were not, after all, cats consecrated to the Devil.[20]

Morris goes on to state how, even after such persecution ended, pure black cats, "or vital parts of them",[21] were thought to have magical, even medicinal qualities. He goes on to tell of several barbaric practices and 'cures', before concluding that their persecution and supposedly healing qualities have made totally black cats incredibly rare indeed. The forebears of our mostly black cats, who have little patches of white or even white whiskers, were the lucky ones who escaped the fires of human persecution.

The torture and killing of cats because of their suspected links to witchcraft and the Devil is a stain on the conscience of humanity. I don't want to spend too long dwelling on what was done to them as this book is for people who love cats and some of the details can be difficult to read. However, I do feel that we owe it to the cats who suffered to acknowledge what was done to them in the name of justice and protection.

> During Lent, cats were thrown onto bonfires or made into scapegoats and driven out of the village boundaries to remove evil from its precincts. In some places a cat was whipped to death to drive evil from the community.[22]

Burning alive seems to have been fate for many an unlucky feline. In some places, "The embers were then collected and taken home to provide luck and protection for the household".[23] Indeed, the remains of cats, whether burned or otherwise, were seen to have protective qualities:

> "...in the Moyse's Museum, Bury St Edmunds, is the mummified body of a kitten or puppy which had been strangled at birth and thrust into a chimney as a magical spell against witchcraft. It was once a fairly common practice to brick a cat or kitten in the wall of a newly constructed house, to provide much the same service against the evil eye. There are examples of such preserved feline cadavers in the museum at Elgin in Scotland".[24]

However, as we are re-learning today, humans can't simply go around destroying what they fear without there being consequences. A terrible threat was heading towards Medieval Europe, more dangerous even than witchcraft. The Black Death was carried by fleas on black rats. Rats were rife in Europe because the cat population had been greatly reduced due to their persecution. Ironically, some people actually believed that cats were the cause of the Black Death and "the Mayor of London ordered that all cats in the areas should be killed",[25] just making the problem worse. The result was devastating.

> In Europe, it is thought that around 50 million people died as a result of the Black Death over the course of three or four years. The population was reduced from some 80 million to 30 million.[26]

While there are some suggestions that plague was being conveyed as an airborne disease rather than purely through flea bites, it seems perfectly sensible to suggest that "you can't spend decades trying to eradicate cats without ecological consequences: in this case more rats. More rats, more fleas, more fleas, more plague".[27]

After centuries of persecution, it is wonderful that we now celebrate the magical associations we have with cats. Many modern practitioners of various Pagan paths find very strong bonds with felines and use them in their magical practice. Deborah Blake's practical text, *The Little Book of Cat Magic*, is a great example of this. It is packed full of spells and magical charms that you can try out, including spells for finding out your cat's name and how not to become a crazy cat person (although, for some of us, it is already too late!). Everything that was once deemed problematic about that connection between the magical practitioner and their familiar is now something in which we can revel.

Yet, if we look back, beyond the burnings, the torture and the accusations, we find a genuine poignancy and sadness. Just imagine a cat or kitten that was managing to eke out a life in a Medieval human settlement. Through no fault of their own, the cat is beaten, kicked, chased out of town. They discover the smell of food wafting out of an open door or window of an isolated house. Inside is a person, usually a woman, who has also been treated with distrust and cruelty by the people of the nearby settlement. The lonely woman strokes the displaced cat. She feeds it. The cat sits on her lap, warms itself by her fire and purrs. Two outcast souls find comfort and respite in each other's company. They form a beautiful loving relationship, a relationship which, in the eyes of their neighbours, is enough to damn them both to the gallows and the flames.

The Witch's Cat, simply by being a cat, ended up revealing the darkest corners, the most barbaric urges, of the human psyche.

Chapter 3

The Cat of the Night – The Knowing Cat

The Knowing Cat by Hannah Willow

In 1977, the Rank Organisation released a movie called *The Uncanny*, a horror portmanteau with cats as the arch villains. In the frame story, a writer called Wilbur Grey, played by horror icon Peter Cushing, tries to persuade his publisher to accept his newest manuscript, a sensational read in which cat are revealed to be evil and manipulative: "We let them prowl around just as they please," Cushing's character laments, "hardly noticing them. And all the time they're watching us, spying on us, making sure that we behave."

Three stories follow, which are given as evidence of the threat that cats pose. In the first, the wealthy Miss Malkin changes her will to leave her fortunes to her cats, cutting out her nephew,

Michael, who arranges for her to be killed by her maid servant, who is then killed and eaten by Miss Malkin's companion cats. In the second tale, the newly orphaned Lucy goes to live with her aunt, where she is tormented by her cousin, Angela. Out of spite, Angela contrives to have Lucy's cat, Wellington, euthanised. Lucy uses her mother's magic books to shrink Angela to a just few inches tall before she is tormented by the resurrected Wellington. In the final story, horror movie actor Valentine De'ath (beautifully overacted by Donald Pleasance) contrives to kill his wife in a seeming accident before moving his new lover into the family home. Confessing his crimes in front of his wife's cat, and then flushing some newborn kittens down the toilet (don't worry, you don't see it!), De'ath is pursued and eventually killed by the feline. "Cat got your tongue?" De'ath's cadaver is asked at the end of the story, before the camera pulls back to reveal that the cat has, indeed, got his tongue and is chewing on it, hungrily. "Cats have been exploiting the human race for centuries," Wilbur Grey announces. "They're the masters!" Moments later, he is lying dead at the bottom of a flight of stairs, having been tripped up by a pack of menacing moggies.

What is really interesting about this film, beyond the usual camp gore of a 1970s British horror, is how it fails, so spectacularly, to make its point that cats are malevolent. In each of the stories, apart from the frame, cats act as the moral centre for the action. It is they who bring punishment to the transgressor; they kill those who conspired against Miss Malkin, make the terrible Valentine De'ath pay for his crimes, and punish the irredeemable Angela. It could be argued that the cats should leave each of these villains to face human justice, but essentially The Uncanny is not a film about how awful cats are; it's a film which reveals how awful people are.

The Knowing Cat does the same – they understand things that humans don't always fully grasp and reveal hidden truths, whether that be the nature of the human psyche, our future or unseen forces at work in the world. The Knowing Cat can not only see clearly in the darkness of night and shadow but can also see through us and in between worlds.

Patricia Dale-Green summed up the Knowing Cat perfectly when she wrote, "The archetypal cat knows its way about our inner world, and can direct us to treasures lying hidden in the recesses of our mind".[1] While this is an interesting and, I think, accurate statement, it is really important that we stop and dismantle a few assumptions before we go any further. As we saw in the last chapter, through a substantial period of western history, cats and the people they lived with were given negative associations and connotations. For Shakespeare, cats were representative of jealousy, "the green-eyed monster which doth mock / the meat it feeds on" (*Othello* 3.3.170-171), alluding to the way that cats seem to torment the prey they have caught. This image suggests a playful malice within the cat's intent. One medieval tale went further, suggesting cats were created by the Devil. The story goes that the Devil became envious of God's creation of humankind and so decided to create a being of his own. He ended up creating the cat, however, it didn't have any fur. It was simply a naked, pink yowling mess of a creature. St Peter looked at the cat and took pity on it. He created the cat's glorious coat, both to keep it warm and to improve its appearance so that humankind would love it. While St Peter's kindness certainly helped the cat, the story still suggests that, at their core, cats are evil and so, perhaps, are we. "Could the story be an allegory of man" Gettings asks, "who is made partly by the Devil and yet will find completion by the Christian message?".[2]

It is interesting how many of these negative associations have followed cats and cat people into the twenty-first century. Probably the most notable of these is the sense of emotional distance which is still ascribed to cats. This attitude can be found everywhere. For example, Gray writes that:

Unlike the dog, who is generally obedient and faithful to its owner, the cat remains an independent and aloof creature. By nature they are solitary: unlike dogs who are pack animals. Cats only want to know you on their terms but they do have a habit of being able to tune into the emotions of humans.[3]

Grey goes further stating that, if a cat's owner dies, they don't mourn or grieve but just move on to the next human or home. We now know that this assertion simply isn't true, and I will be challenging this stereotype more fully in the next chapter, but what is interesting is just how pervasive this belief is and how it is also applied to people who have cats in their home. For example, Jessica Dawn Palmer states that cat people:

...are introspective and listen to their own intelligence. A cat person is unlikely to heed other people's advice, no matter how good it is or well-intended. Indeed, they appear a trifle self-indulgent and extremely self-absorbed. The cat person tends to be slender, graceful, well-turned out and vain.[4]

As far as I'm aware, this does not describe me (I don't believe I have ever been described as either 'slender' nor 'graceful') and it certainly doesn't describe the cat lovers and enthusiasts I know, who are generally very warm and considerate people.

In his wonderful book, *The Secret Lore of Cats*, Gettings moves beyond such sweeping generalisations but suggest that one of the reasons why cats are such beloved pets is that we see ourselves reflected in them. He states that, on a species-wide level:

The reason why the cat has such an attraction for the human being is because the cat represents a densification of a part of the human soul which was beautiful as well as cruel ... When we look at other animals, we look at discarded elements of a previous self – we look towards our past. When we look at a cat, we have a glimpse of the inner potential of the human soul for grace, as though we look towards the future.[5]

He then takes a step closer, looking at the relationship between an individual and their pet, seeing the same sense of the reflected self:

> …it is not unusual to find a spiritual correlation between the psyches of pet and owner … Some [cats] are almost mirrors of their owner's spiritual life or state of mind. A spiritually troubled owner rarely has a peaceful feline: show me a contented cat and I will show you a peaceful owner.[6]

In a final step, Gettings questions whether our cats are merely externalised fragments of our inner life staring back at us. He doesn't really settle on an answer, but my answer to this question is quite clear – no, they aren't. I find this approach too human-centric, too self-centred. Cats are individual beings and are not on Earth to merely reflect us or our emotional state. They have their own lives, their own purpose. Their existence is not all about reflecting humanity, although they can help us on our spiritual journeys.

One of the ways that Gettings suggests that cats, and other pets, can help us access the "higher level in the human psyche"[7] is by helping us to experience perhaps the most beautiful quality of all: "those who actively love their pets, and attempt to establish a harmonious relationship with animals, are already learning the secrets of universal love".[8] I don't feel this is a point I really need to expand upon with further written sources as I am sure many readers will understand this completely. The relationships we build with our cats often feel transcendent and unconditional. We love them, or so it feels, with our whole heart. For example, I remember meeting up with a group of friends I hadn't seen in about a decade. Many were married and bought their spouses. As we ate, they told us about their children and family lives. When it was my turn, I explained that I didn't have any children but I did have two cats. Suddenly, the table erupted in warmth and humour. Everyone got out their phones to show me pictures of their cat and regaled the table with stories of their antics. Although they all, obviously, loved their children, it was the love of their cats which brought a commonality and unity to that gathering.

It is not only universal love which cats can help us access. Jung believed that there was an inner cat which humans could contact through our collective unconscious. As he felt that the cat was predominantly associated with the feminine aspect, "Jung felt it was [especially] productive for his male patients to work with this inner cat".[9] Many practitioners may try to access the energy of felines when they work with them as totem or power animals, while, similarly, those involved in shamanic practices work with "an archetypal representative of all cats".[10]

So, when we begin working with these archetypal energies, where do they lead us? Gettings positions the archetypal cat as a magical and deeply perceptive creature that is absolutely central to the human spiritual experience. He states that:

> ...the cat sits brooding over the deep well of hidden wisdom in every human soul. She made herself guardian of this secret pool of wisdom, and was at the very beginning of our recorded history worshipped as a goddess.[11]

This idea of accessing the 'pool of wisdom' is developed further by Philip and Stephanie Carr-Gomm in *The Druid Animal Oracle*, as they suggest the cat shows us the way to access deeper truths.

> The cat unites an awareness of the spirit-world with a highly developed sensuality. These two attributes are not polar opposites as dualistic spiritual teachings would have us

believe, but are facets of one continuum of awareness and sensitivity. Working towards wholeness involves enhancing our appreciation of both physical and non-physical worlds.[12]

It is this suggestion, of the cat "at once centred in its own being yet at the same time clearly enmeshed in the spiritual realm"[13], that I advocate in this book and in working with the Cat of the Night and the Cat of the Day. Cats are, indeed, deeply spiritual beings but they also like rolling in catnip and chasing butterflies. They don't just sit in meditation but connect very deeply with their senses as they explore the world around them. The Knowing Cat encourages us to do the same.

One recurring belief about cats is that they have a sixth sense; a sense of premonition or what is to come. Much folklore has developed around the world which tells of the cats' ability to predict the future. Normally these come in the shape of omens, with the appearance of a cat in a particular situation foretelling an event. It is also believed that cats could predict the weather:

> ...in America if a cat sits with its back to the fire then we are heading for a cold snap; the same is said if a cat sleeps with all four paws tucked under its body. If they wash inside and around their ears, then rain will be upon us within the day or most certainly the next.[14]

While some of these 'predictions' may be a little broad (cats wash around their ears regularly, so if you live in a place prone to rain then this will likely come true at some point), cats seem to be capable of predicting major geological events, such as earthquakes. It has been suggested that this could be due to changes in the Earth's magnetic field. Morris notes that "Similar responses have been recorded when cats have predicted volcanic eruptions or severe electrical storms".[15] There is also some evidence that cats may be able to predict tsunamis.

Among several recorded stories of such predictions is that of Toto, a cat who lived with his human family close to Mount Vesuvius in the 1940s. While most attention at that time was focused on the destruction caused by World War Two, Toto was attuned to more natural phenomena. On March 17th 1944, Toto began scratching the face of his sleeping male human. Realising that this wasn't Toto's usual behaviour, the man woke up the rest of his family. After a short discussion, they decided to take Toto's warning seriously and left their village. Only an hour after, Mount Vesuvius erupted and their village was buried in lava.[16]

In addition to natural phenomena, cats seem to be able to predict events which are more human focused. For example, there is anecdotal evidence that cats can sense when their humans are about to arrive home. Dr Rupert Sheldrake investigated this phenomenon and generated some interesting findings:

> The survey of 1,200 households showed that over half (55 per cent) of … dogs could regularly anticipate the return of their owners while the figure for cats demonstrating the same talent was a lowly 30 per cent. But, as Sheldrake points out, this does not necessarily mean dogs are better at it. It could simply be that cats don't care as much.[17]

Cats' lack of regard for humans was also revealed in "a 2013 study which found that cats do recognize their owners' voices, but choose to ignore them".[18] While this may be hurtful to our feelings, I'm sure cat lovers aren't surprised by these findings. Maybe that Chinese creation myth, where cats couldn't be bothered to look after the world, was not so far-fetched after all!

Beyond natural phenomena and the arrival of their humans, there are also several compelling stories of cats being able to predict events which really do suggest that they have psychic abilities. These stories are anecdotal but create a real sense of magic around our feline friends.

Just like Toto's warning, mentioned above, the following example happened during the turbulent days of World War Two. Faith was a stray cat who was adopted by the staff at St Augustine and St Faith's Church, close to St Paul's Cathedral, in London in the late 1930s. In August of 1940, Faith had a single male black and white kitten, who became known as Panda. In early September of that year, Faith became increasingly agitated and repeatedly took Panda down into the basement of the church, hiding him away in a corner. No matter how many times the staff members bought Panda back up, Faith insisted on carrying him back down into the secluded corner of the church's basement. On 9th September 1940, St Augustine and St Faith's Church was almost totally destroyed in a German air raid. As the rubble was cleared, Faith and Panda were found, not only safe but completely unharmed in the ruins of the basement. A sign for parishioners stated:

"Shielding her kitten in a sort of recess in the house (a spot she selected three days before the tragedy occurred), [Faith] sat the whole frightful night on bombing and fire, guarding her little kitten".[19]

The only explanations for Faith's behaviour are either some sort of precognition or total coincidence. Being a firm believer in the magic of cats, I know which explanation I prefer.

Many people believe that cats not only see the future but can also see ghosts and spirits of the dead. How many times has your cat stopped what they were doing and suddenly looked behind you or stared into a space where there seems to be nothing happening? We often stop and look to see if we can glimpse what has caught their attention but, more often than not, there is nothing there. This has led to the suspicion that they are in fact seeing ghosts or echoes of the past.

What is, perhaps, more interesting is that "the most common

forms of spirit phenomena seen in houses are ghostly cats".[20] There are numerous reports of different ghost cats but one of the most famous is of the white cat belonging to Mrs Winge who lived in Congleton, Cheshire in the nineteenth century. She reported that her cat came home one day, as normal, and sat on the front step. When she encouraged the cat to come in, the feline simply disappeared. It became clear that the cat had died at some point during the day and it was the spirit or ghost of the white cat which returned home. The same happened the next day, and the next. Mrs Whinge even asked her neighbours to come and visit and they also reported seeing the cat return home before disappearing as it crossed the threshold. There were reports well into the twentieth century of a small white cat sitting in the vicinity of the property, which disappeared when approached by passers-by.[21]

Reports of ghostly cats reinforce the sense that there is something supernatural about them, that they can connect with and contact worlds inaccessible to humans. For example, in the Celtic tradition, cats are seen as "magical creatures with links to the faerie kingdom ... According to Celtic folklore, the Cat Sidhe (Irish) and Cat Sith (Scots) were faeries in the form of large black cats with a single white spot on their chest"[22] that "allow themselves to be glimpsed, to remind us of the existence of the Otherworld".[23] Here, again, we begin to feel the influence of the Universal Cat, who is far more ancient and powerful than the human mind can grasp.

The Universal Cat, the Witch's Cat and the Knowing Cat, are all one and the same thing. They are different aspects of the Cat of the Night, an unknowable, shadowy and mystical being that has intrigued humanity for centuries. Yet our relationship with the Cat of the Night has been as changeable as both the Moon and the pupil of the cat.

Deep down, we know that our cats know more than us, are connected to the world in ways that we cannot comprehend.

We look into their eyes and we see an inherent understanding far beyond our own. This sense of connection is beautifully expressed in Pattiann Rogers' poem *Finding the cat in a spring field at midnight*. Across the poem, Rogers argues that "It takes a peculiar vision to be able to detect / Precisely where" a range of vividly drawn elemental images, such as "the spring / Stars slinking past the eyes of midnight", "End / And the cat begins."24 Rogers' cat is so deeply connected to the natural and the universal that our human senses cannot distinguish them.

Centuries ago, in ancient Egypt, the sense of knowing and connection Rogers explores was deified and worshipped in temples. In more recent times, it has led to a sense of distrust and persecution as our frail human egos demanded that beings with such intelligence must be evil. Today, as science begins to work out quite why cats seem so much more attuned to the world than we are, we can finally appreciate them for who and what they really are.

To do so we must bring them out of the darkness of myth and superstition. We must bring them out of the light of the Moon and into the daylight. And in doing so, we find a whole other kind of magic in our cats.

We are discovering, or rather rediscovering, The Cat of the Day.

The Cat of the Day

Who is The Cat of the Day?

The Cat of the Day by Hannah Willow

So, the Cat of the Day with the pink, pink nose,
With a dark stripey back and bright golden toes,
Was a gift to the Earth, as a sign of great love,
From her Firey Father in the bright sky above.

In my poem, the Cat of the Day is the embodiment of daytime and daylight, who falls out of the crown of the Sun. As he runs around the Earth, he brings illumination with him, the beauty of a winter's sunrise and the harmony of a drowsy summer's evening. He ushers in not only the day time but the light half of the year, when "daytimes are longer and bright". The Sun, proud of his glorious golden creation, looks down from the sky as the Cat of the Day brings warmth and plenty to the Earth.

While we tend to associate cats with the Moon, they also have very strong connections to solar energy and Sun gods. The most notable of these solar connections is the Egyptian Sun god Ra, who appeared in the form of the great cat, Mau, to protect the Tree of Life and kill the serpent Apep. The cat-bodied Great Sphinx of Giza faces east towards the rising Sun and was believed to guard this world against the Otherworld, which arrived with the darkness of night. The cat also brings in solar energy through its association with the star sign Leo, whose ruling planet is the Sun. This is why, in my poem, the Sun breathes golden light onto the belly of the Cat of the Day, making him glow with solar energy. It also means that the figure more closely resembles my own cat, Alfie, a glorious marmalade tabby. Alfie has always seemed to me to be the physical embodiment of the Sun, and not just because of his deep golden colouring. He is a complete Sun worshipper. In the depths of winter, he will seek out the smallest patch of sunlight to lay in. Even on the hottest days of the year, Alfie will find a place in direct sunlight, usually rolling onto his back to get a toasty tummy. He seems to, somehow, drink in the energy of the sunshine and his coat becomes even more lustrous and golden as a result.

In just the same way as the first rays of sunlight on the Winter Solstice call us to wake from our slumber, the Cat of the Day challenges us to question everything we think we know about cats. This is a challenge we should take. After all, the cat has always been associated with change, notably in the ways their eyes react to light. However, while this change has long been associated with the phases of the Moon, changes in the size of a cat's pupils is actually triggered by the cycle of the Sun. In the bright light of day, cat's pupils are thin horizontal lines; as the Sun sets and there is less light, a cat's pupils grow wider.

As we begin to challenge our assumptions, other, somewhat stereotypical beliefs, also come into question. The idea that cats are "aloof" and "only want to know you on their terms"[1] is simply not true. Of course, some cats are like that but by no means all. Alfie is a very friendly feline and walks up to household visitors, with his tail in the air, to greet them. He is never happier than when all four members of our household are in the same room and chatting to each other. In fact, he is a wonderful cat at bringing people together. This was most notable in the first few days after we got him, where he introduced himself to all our friends, while seeming happy to accept that Marlowe was in charge. The pair soon became an inseparable and finely tuned team.

The role that cats play within our households is also changing and, consequently, cats' behaviour is evolving because of the expectations of their humans. Whereas, once, we needed them to be keen and focused predators, helping keep our homes free from vermin, this is no longer the case. Cats still show aspects of hunting behaviour, perhaps bringing home prey and presenting it to their owners. Alfie is not such a fearless hunter and recently ran away from a particularly large spider we were hoping he would catch for us. He will, however, retrieve a drinking straw or scrunched up crisp packet if it is thrown for him! Within twenty-first century households, cats tend to play the role of "an overgrown kitten"[2] rather than a hunter, being cuddled, fussed and eating treats.

The joy of living with cats has echoed down the centuries with many notable or famous cat owners sharing wonderful stories about their feline friends. Those of us lucky enough to live with cats get to see their intelligence and invention up close. For example, one Christmas Eve, we discovered that Alfie was able to open our fridge. We had bought a very fresh and very expensive turkey for a family gathering and found Alfie on the top shelf, straddling the sizeable bird and helping himself to our Christmas dinner. What was even more interesting was when Marlowe discovered that Alfie could open the fridge. He used to get Alf to climb up onto the shelves and drop stolen treats down onto the floor for him. Eventually, we had to replace the fridge for one with a cat-proof door.

Their evolving roles within our homes has also changed how we think about cats. The twenty-first-century view of cats is very different from that even fifty years ago. For example, female cats had the reputation for being highly sexed, to the point where prostitutes were known as 'alley cats' and brothels were colloquially known as the 'cat house'. However, with neutering now far more common, this association is changing, although an echo of it survives in the naming of a sexually voracious older woman as a 'cougar'. Generally, how we think about cats has become more positive.

The Cat of the Day brings all our assumptions and associations into the clear light of the Sun. He gets us to look again at what we think we know about cats and ask ourselves if it is really true. He pulls us out of our daydreams, our distractions and our meditations and gets us to focus on the here and now. He demands that we be present in the moment. Alfie hates my mobile phone. If I spend too long looking at the screen, he appears somewhere in my eyeline and glares at me until I put it down. He knows that I can get lost in virtual worlds and how damaging that can be, so he brings me out of it. He has also been known to interrupt meditations and rituals, drawing me away from the mystical and esoteric and getting me to focus on the physical world.

Once present, we can fully appreciate just how wonderful our cats are. As a physical, biological entity, cats are simply amazing. I am always stunned to see that, even at the grand old age of seventeen, Alfie can jump a six-foot fence from a seated position on the ground. He has a physicality and an agility which is, frankly, awe inspiring. He also has the deepest, loudest rumbly purr of any cat I have ever met. I believe his purr is profoundly magical and has healing properties far beyond any supposed healing spell or ritual. Maybe this explains why I fall asleep with him purring away beside me so often.

However, Alfie has another magical quality which has provided the inspiration for the next chapter of this book. Alfie is a talker. He talks all the time (apart from when we went to an Animal Communicator when he didn't have much to say at all). Alfie has different sounds for different occasions. He makes a trilling noise when he walks into a room. He will answer back if you chat to him. He even has distinct names for me, Becky and Marlowe, so you know exactly who he is talking about. Alfie's skill as a communicator led me to realise how the magic of cats has seeped into our language and the stories we tell each other. This is a conscious kind of magic we use every day.

And that is the perfect place to begin our journey to explore a different kind of cat magic, one which is rooted in the apparent, physical world around us, which we find in our words, our homes and our hearts. This is the magic of the Cat of the Day.

Chapter 4

The Cat of the Day – The Idiomatic Cat

The Idiomatic Cat by Hannah Willow

Once upon a time, there was a Miller who had three possessions: a mill, a donkey and a cat. When he died, the Miller's sons split their inheritance between them. The eldest son got the mill and took over his father's profession. The second son got the donkey and made his living transporting goods for people. The third and youngest son inherited the cat. Disappointed with his inheritance, the youngest son moaned, "What good will this cat do me? My brothers will be able to earn a living with their inheritances and all I can do is cook and eat this cat! Then I shall be hungry again! Oh, I am so unlucky!"

Overhearing the young man, the cat turned to him and said, "Don't worry, master. If you can get me a sack and a pair of boots, I'll make you far wealthier than either of your brothers." After recovering from the shock of discovering that he had a talking cat, and that the cat wanted boots and not a bowl of fish, the young man followed the cat's instructions and gave him both a sack and a lovely pair of boots to wear.

By now, this story should be sounding familiar. Today we know it as *Puss in Boots*, a character that has gained renewed interest in the twenty-first century after he appeared in the *Shrek* franchise. He is an example of an Idiomatic Cat, a figure that has embedded itself in our language and our stories. The Idiomatic Cat is different to the Universal Cat that we find in myth and legend because they do not deal with grand universal truths, stars and planets, gods and goddesses. They deal with humans, the interactions we have and the situations we find ourselves in every day. These cats are no less potent than their Universal counterparts, but their magic is very different.

The version of the *Puss in Boots* story that most of us know was published by Charles Perrault in 1697, although there is an older version of the story in Italian by Giovanni Francesco Straparola from the 1550s. It is ultimately thought to be derived from an Indian folk tale which can be found in the fifth century text *Panchatantra*.[1] What is interesting about this story is that while Puss has some features of the Cat of the Night (notably that he is something of a trickster and isn't entirely honest), he operates in a very different way. There is no magic involved in what he does, nor does he use other otherworldly energies or beings to bring his plans to life. He creates success purely by being immersed in and understanding how to work the apparent, material world.

Once he had his sack (and his highly fashionable pair of boots), Puss set about catching a series of small animals and birds, which he presented to the King on behalf of his master. However, rather than saying he worked for a Miller's son, Puss said that his master was the Marquis of Carabas. Hearing that the King will be driving by with his beautiful daughter, Puss arranged for his feckless master to be bathing in a river and pretended that the young man's clothes had been stolen. Thinking he was dealing with the Marquis of Carabas, the King presented the young man with a highly expensive new outfit, meaning he looked like a Marquis. Puss pulled further tricks to make the King believe that the Marquis of Carabas had lots of land and ultimately tricked an ogre out of his castle. Thinking that the young man was a good match, the King offered his daughter's hand in marriage and they all live happily and wealthily ever after, even Puss in Boots, who was made a lord of the realm. At the end of her version of Perrault's tale, Angela Carter makes the moral of the story explicit: "A great inheritance may be a fine thing; but hard work and ingenuity will take a young man further than his father's money".[2]

There is another storybook cat who elevates his master above his humble beginnings, although he doesn't need boots, nor an elaborate scheme, to do so. This cat creates success simply doing what cats do.

In the medieval English tale, young Richard, or rather Dick, Whittington went to London because he thought the streets were paved with gold. Instead, he found they were swarming with rats. Taking employment with a merchant called Fitzwarren, Dick found himself living in a rat-infested house until, with his first wages, he bought himself a cat. The cat soon cleared the house of all the rats and Dick could finally sleep comfortably. Fitzwarren planned a trading expedition to Morocco and convinced Dick to let him take the cat on the ship, to help keep the rats at bay. Once the expedition had set off, rats swarmed back into the house and made Dick's life a misery. He considered fleeing the city but returned after hearing Bow Bells call out to him: "Turn again Whittington, Thrice Mayor of London".[3] Meanwhile, Fitzwarren's trading expedition arrived at its destination to find that Morocco was also overrun with rats. Fitzwarren lent the ruler of Morocco Whittington's cat, which instantly cleared the palace of the vermin. The ruler of Morocco offered Fitzwarren a fortune for the cat but he refused. Instead, he sold him several kittens that had been born on the journey. Arriving home, Fitzwarren gave Whittington his cat back, as well as all the money the ruler of Morocco had paid for the kittens. Dick married Fitzwarren's daughter, Alice, and, just as the bells prophesised, became the Lord Mayor of London three times. They all, including the cat, lived happily ever after.

The story of Dick Whittington and his cat continues to be an incredibly popular tale, particularly around Christmas when it is frequently performed as a pantomime. The story is based in historical fact, although there is a notable character missing:

> [Richard Whittington] was born about 1357 at Pauntley in Gloucestershire, the youngest son of Sir William Whittington, who died soon afterwards. In his early teens he went to London to be apprenticed to Sir Ivo Fitz Waryn, a wealthy mercer whose daughter he later married: he built up a substantial fortune as a merchant, held high office in the Mercer's Guild, and was three times elected as Mayor of London.[4]

This begs the question – where's the cat? Dick's cat is absolutely central to this story and, on stage, is the character with whom the children in the audience engage with most fully. Well, unfortunately, he probably didn't have a cat at all.

> It has been pointed out that since Whittington rose to power through purchase or bribery, and that such profitable enterprise was in those days called 'achat' (though French, it was seemingly pronounced in those times with a hard c, to give the sound 'acat') the confusion between 'acat' and 'a cat' is understandable in later expansions of the rags-to-riches story.[5]

However, it doesn't really matter if his cat was real or not, because the story is so well known that the cat has ended up gaining somewhat legendary status. A statue of a cat sits on a mile stone on Highgate Hill, supposedly marking the point at which Whittington turned back to London, and, when the church where Whittington is buried was damaged by a bomb in 1944:

> ...a mummified cat was found among the wreckage ... the workmen repairing the church were naturally convinced that this must be Whittington's own original cat – or, at the very least, a cat placed in his tomb when this was restored after the [Great Fire of London] in 1666".[6]

Real or not, Whittington's cat is a true Idiomatic Cat, one whose transformative magic is entirely grounded in real world cat behaviour.

To find our next Idiomatic Cat we need to go to Japan, specifically to the Gotokuji temple in Tokyo. One day the temple was visited by the Emperor, but all was not well. Dark clouds gathered over the ornate building and beautiful gardens. A storm was on its way. As the Emperor followed the path through the site, something caught his eye. In the doorway of one of the buildings was a cat and it seemed to be waving at him. Looking more closely, the Emperor realized the cat wasn't waving but beckoning, telling him to come closer. Intrigued, the Emperor moved towards the doorway where the cat was sitting. Suddenly, there was a brilliant flash and a bolt of lightning struck the very spot where the Emperor had been standing. Once he had recovered from the shock, the Emperor realized that the beckoning cat had saved his life and that he had been very lucky to escape.[7]

There is a variant of this story where the cat of a Buddhist Monk encounters a group of Samurai sheltering under a tree during a storm and beckons to them to follow it, just before the tree is struck by lightning. As a result of the cat's actions, the land on which the Gotokuji temple now stands was gifted to the Monk and his cat.[8]

Despite the variations of the story, the result was the

same; cats became a symbol of good luck in Japan. Japanese craftspeople created the Maneki Neko, a figurine of a Cat with a single moving arm. Ceramic examples of such figurines can be found as early as the Edo period (between 1603-1867) and, today, mass produced versions are found all around the world. To westerners, it looks like the cat is waving, but that is not the case at all. The name, Maneki Neko, translates as 'beckoning cat' and the figure is, in fact, beckoning good luck towards it, just as the cat had done to the Emperor and the Samurai.

All three of these Idiomatic cats bring good luck and some kind of material reward to their humans, whether that be wealth and riches, as in *Puss in Boots* or Dick Whittington, or the gift of a piece of land. They are also all related in one way or another to people of high status. Whittington's cat impressed the ruler of Morocco and helped Whittington become the Lord Mayor, the cat of the Gotokuji temple beckons Samurai or even the Emperor to follow it, while Puss in Boots talks directly to the King. These figures remind us of an old idiomatic phrase which has an unknown origin.

During the croquet game in *Alice's Adventures in Wonderland*, the King of Hearts finds the Cheshire Cat gazing at him:

'Don't be impertinent,' said the King, 'and don't look at me like that!' He got behind Alice as he spoke.
'A cat may look at a king,' said Alice. 'I've read that in some book, but I don't remember where'.[9]

The phrase 'a cat may look at a king' is an example of an idiom, a phrase which is understood by speakers of a language or people of a certain culture, although the meaning is not clear purely through the words itself. Understanding an idiom comes through the accepted, repeated usage of the phrase by people and by examining the image or picture it creates. So, what are we meant to understand by the idiom 'a cat may look at a king'?

Well, in the phrase, the king is obviously someone of very high status. The cat represents the opposite, being a lowly, somewhat overlooked figure. The phrase is first recorded in print in a work by John Heywood in 1546, when most domestic cats would have been working animals, hunting household vermin. In that sense, this idiom can be taken to mean that even the lowest figure in a society has some rights. This meaning was made more explicit when the phrase was used and developed by the writer Robert Greene in 1590: "A Cat may looke at a King, and a swaynes eye hath as high a reach as a Lords looke".[10] In this extension of the idiom, a swayne is a peasant. Again, we see a figure of low birth seen in relation to a character of higher status. Similar phrases can be found in other languages: "The same image is found in the German and Italian phrases: sieht doch die Katze den Kaiser an and un gatto può ben guardare un re",[11] while equivalent Spanish and French phrases use dogs instead of cats.

One of the issues with idioms which involve cats is that they may not be referring to a cat at all. The phrase 'there isn't enough room to swing a cat', meaning that there isn't very much space, is a prime example. The image that it recalls is, frankly, horrifying: that of an unsuspecting feline being grasped by the tail and whirled around above someone's head. Thankfully, that is not the case at all. The idiom refers to a cat-o'-nine-tails, a particularly gruesome whip which was made up of nine strands, each with a knot at the end. Such whips were used to punish sailors. Inside ships there wasn't enough space to brandish the whip and so the sailors had their punishment administered on the deck. Therefore, below decks, there wasn't enough room to swing the 'cat'. Although this idiom does not directly reference felines, there is a cat association with the name of the whip, "because it left scars on the backs of the whipped sailors reminiscent of the claw marks of a savage cat".[12]

It's also possible that the idiom 'let the cat out of the bag', meaning to reveal a secret, also references the cat-o'-nine tails.

Some claim that the phrase comes from the tradition on ships of storing the whip in a sack, then taking it out before the punishment was administered. However, this doesn't seem to fit the meaning of the phrase as presumably, when the whip was taken out of the bag, the sailor would have already known they were going to be whipped, therefore, it wouldn't have been much of a surprise.

A more likely origin of this phrase refers to a deceptive practice involving buying and selling animals:

> Piglets were often taken to market in a small sack, or bag, to be sold. The trickster would put a cat in the bag and pretend that it was a pig. If the buyer insisted on seeing it, he would be told that it was too lively to risk opening up the bag, as the animal might escape. If the cat struggled so much that the trickster let the cat out of the bag, his secret was exposed. A popular name for the bag itself was a 'poke', hence that other expression 'never buy a pig in a poke'.[13]

While some have cast doubt on whether this trick could work (presumably a cat in a sack would make a noise very different to that of a piglet), the 'pig in a poke' idiom does seem to add legitimacy to this reading, as do version of this idiom in both "Dutch – 'Een kat in de zak kopen' and in German – 'Die Katze im Sack kaufen'. These both translate loosely as 'to buy a cat in a bag', that is, to buy false goods.".[14]

Sometimes, idioms gain such widespread usage that they change. Bits of them get clipped, left off or dropped, so that they appear to make even less sense. This is the case with the idiom 'not a cat in Hell's chance', which means to have no realistic chance of success in a situation. For me, this phrase raises several questions: why is the cat in Hell in the first place and why doesn't it have a chance of success? A similar phrase, about not having 'a snowball's chance in Hell' is clearer, because the ice-cold snowball would melt in the fiery flames of Hell. To discover why the cat doesn't have a chance in hell, we need to go back to when the phrase was first used. This was on 29th September 1753, when *Jackson's Oxford Journal* wrote an account of a prisoner "Poor John Billingsgate"[15] who had his tongue cut out as punishment for his crimes. In a note, Billingsgate wrote that "Without a Tongue I have no more chance in Life, than a Cat in Hell without Claws".[16] In other words, he had no way of defending himself. It wasn't until later that the two words 'without claws' was dropped as the idiom became streamlined.

One of the most well-known idioms involving felines is the phrase 'it's raining cats and dogs', meaning that it is raining very heavily:

> The phrase became popular several centuries ago at a time when the streets of towns were narrow, filthy and had poor drainage. Unusually heavy storms produced torrential flooding which drowned large numbers of the half-starved cats and dogs that foraged there. After a downpour was over, people would emerge from their houses to find the corpses of these unfortunate animals, and the more gullible among them believed that the bodies must have fallen from the sky – and that it had literally been raining cats and dogs".[17]

Some linguists change the context of this slightly, stating how, in bad weather, feral animals would take shelter in the straw of thatched roofs and would, therefore, be swept off them the rain was particularly heavy.

All these idiomatic expressions show cats in desperate situations. They are portrayed as the lowest members of society, victims of extreme weather and market-place deceptions, left helpless and unable to defend themselves. Where is the magical, lucky, Idiomatic Cat, such as those discussed in stories at the start of this chapter? Well, thankfully they do appear in our language and phraseology too, most notably when we consider just how lucky cats are. The belief or saying that a cat has nine lives reflects specifically on the cat's ability to escape from difficult situations. However, the number nine has magical qualities relating to a range of different faiths and beliefs. Morris suggests that the number nine was special because, in Christian belief, "it was a 'trinity of trinities' and therefore ideally suited the 'lucky' cat".[18] Franklin suggests that the number nine relates to "the magical number of the Goddess, the three aspects of the moon goddess tripled and the number of months of a human pregnancy"[19] while Gettings connects it to the nine deities of Heliopolis in Ancient Egypt "Atum, Shu, Tefnut, Geb, Nut, Osiris, Isis, Set and Nephthys, each of which was linked in some way with the cat".[20] Whichever explanation we choose, its connection with the number nine shows us that the Idiomatic Cat is incredibly fortuitous.

There is a sense in which language around cats has become more positive over time. For example, a version of the phrase 'curiosity killed the cat' was first used by Ben Johnson in his play *Every Man in his Humor* in 1598 and seems to stand as a warning against being overly inquisitive. However, in the twentieth century, there was an attempt to change the phrase, to encourage, rather than chide people for being curious. This version of the saying reads 'curiosity killed the cat, but satisfaction brought it back'. This attempt to alter the meaning was so successful that it is now often cited as the original meaning of the phrase.[21] Similarly positive terms, such as 'the cat's whiskers', 'the cat's meow' and even 'the cat's pyjamas', as ways of describing something or someone as high quality were coined in the United States in the optimistic and playful decade of the 1920s.[22] And let us not forget the swinging sixties, when the greatest compliment was to be called a 'cool cat'.

However, for me, the most magical words connected to cats, are the words we use for them. Take the actual word 'cat', for example. It is such a small word, just three letters, and one which we use so often, that it is easy for us to overlook. However, this tiny little everyday word connects us with cat lovers around the world and right the way back to the ancient world:

> The name 'cat' is used in almost every European nation with a slight variation: in French, *chat*; German, *Katze*; Italian, *gatto*; Spanish, *gato*; Swedish, *katt*; Norwegian, *katt*; Dutch, *Kat*; Icelandic, *kottur*; Polish, *kot*; It is also found in countries around the Mediterranean: in Yiddish it is *kats*, in Greek, *gata*, and in Maltese *qattus*. Clearly, this is an ancient word that has spread across the world from a single source. The source appears to be Arabic, because the oldest use of it is found in North Africa, where it is *quttah*.[23]

Similarly, one of our affectionate terms for felines, and name of that fashionably booted, Idiomatic cat discussed at the start of the chapter, also has ancient roots. The word Puss "is almost certainly from the Egyptian word *pasht*, which was one of the names of the goddess Bastet"[24].

However, my favourite cat word is one we have already used in connection with the Cat of the Day, the name of the great God Ra's cat alter-ego – Mau. "The word "Mau" translates from the Egyptian language, both as 'light' and as 'cat'"[25]. What I think is so wonderful about this word, beyond connecting cats with the light of the Sun, is that it sounds just like the noise cats make: Meow. Isn't it wonderful to think that one day, many centuries ago, someone was wondering what to call a cat and named it after the sound coming out of their mouths? Or, perhaps, even more magically, cats started making that sound because humans kept saying the word to them. Whichever way you look at it, what more magical name could we wish for the Idiomatic Cat than the one it gives itself whenever it speaks to us?

Chapter 5

The Cat of the Day – The Physical Cat

The Physical Cat by Hannah Willow

As we have seen, the traditional figure of the Cat of the Night is considered by many to have supernatural abilities, such as being able to predict the future and detect the presence of ghosts and spirits. Along with such skills, their changeable, Moon-like eyes and their sense of independence has marked cats out as creatures of the Otherworld, potent beings with whom magical practitioners have worked for centuries. While I in no way want to sweep aside this archetypal figure, I would like to suggest that it is time that our assessment of cat's magical abilities evolved. As we begin to work with the Cat of the Day and the more practical, earthy energies of the Idiomatic Cat, a more holistic approach to their magical qualities in needed.

As we take the cat out of the shadowy, superstitious world of the night and put them into the clear, bright light of day we can see that many of their supposedly magical qualities emanate from their natural, physical bodies. Cats' senses are much sharper and more attuned than ours. For example, when they stop and stare into an empty space, it is entirely likely that they have seen a small movement or heard a faint creak from the structure of the building, something that our less precise human senses failed to pick up. Similarly, while cats may seem to be able to predict events, perhaps their whiskers have picked up changes in the air flow or they have detected an electromagnetic change that eluded their human counterparts.

Once we see cats' abilities in this way, we may well ask ourselves whether or not it makes cats any less magical. Does it rob them of their special status and reduce them to a mere physical automaton? My response to these questions would be a resounding "No". In fact, for me, seeing the cat in this way makes them even more magical. It means that magic isn't just something intangible and or elusive, it is something right in front of us, a force we can observe and appreciate in our everyday lives. The cat who sits on your doorstep and curls up on your lap for a cuddle is a wonder of biological and evolutionary process. Appreciating the marvels of the Physical Cat in your home is an important step in realising that cats really are as magical as we have always believed them to be.

Let's begin by taking a few steps back along the evolutionary ladder to trace where our modern, domesticated cats came from:

Felines originally evolved between 65-33 million years ago from a species known as miacids – long-toothed, tree-climbing carnivorous mammals. These creatures were intelligent hunters with the sharp teeth and claws to enable them to catch and eat their prey. This species splits into two groups, and we can trace the ancestors of modern cats back about 11 million years with the emergence of the sub-species *panthera* (roaring cat), *acinonyx* (cheetah) and *felis* (all other small cats).[1]

The cats that now live in our homes are descended from populations of African wildcats which were found in and around Egypt, North Africa and the Near East called the *Felis sylvestris lybica*. Domestic cats belong to the classification of *Felis catus*, although, as Brennan writes, they have much in common with their ancestors:

> The basic design of the cat – supple, low-slung body, long tail, a hunter's teeth and claws – which appeared in the early Pliocene, proved so successful that it has remained more or less unchanged to the present day.[2]

If we consider what Brennan calls a domestic cat's "basic design" – their supple, agile bodies – then we will see that they truly are magical creatures. Cats have a free-floating clavicle, or collarbone, which allows them to get through any space where they can fit their head. The clavicle connects the cat's shoulders to their forelegs, which means they have a great deal of agility and can position their forelegs in almost any direction. Cats can jump up to seven times their own height, which enables them to scale higher vantage points where they can more easily see their prey. However, they aren't so good at getting down from such heights: "The reason is that their claws face backwards. This simple anatomical fact means your cat can climb a tree as nimbly as a spider, but has to come down backwards in short, ungainly jumps".[3] This can mean that cats need rescuing, evoking the stereotype of the Fire Service being called to get a cat out of a tree. Alternatively, they may fall. However, the magical Physical Cat also has a way of coping with that.

Between the ages of three to four weeks old, cats develop their 'righting reflex' which means that they are able to twist their bodies and give themselves a better chance of landing safely when they fall. Desmond Morris describes this process in detail, showing just how complex it actually is:

> As it starts to fall, with its body upside-down, an automatic twisting reaction begins at the head end of the body. The head rotates first, until it is upright, then the front legs are brought up close to the face, ready to protect it from impact. (A blow to a cat's chin from underneath can be particularly serious.) Next, the upper part of the spine is twisted, bringing the front half of the body round in line with the head. Finally, the hind legs are bent up, so that all four limbs are now ready for touchdown and, as this happens, the cat twists the rear half of its body round to catch up with the front. Finally, as it is about to make contact, it stretches all four legs out towards the ground and arches its back, as a way of reducing the force of the impact.
>
> While this body-twisting is taking place, the stiffened tail is rotating like a propellor, acting as a counterbalancing device. All of this occurs in a fraction of a second and it requires slow-motion film to analyse these rapid stages of the righting response.[4]

What Morris describes here is only part of the way that cats lessen the impact of a fall, as there are a range of other physical factors, including spreading out their body, which helps to reduce their velocity. To some people this may just be a simple physical response, an example of the physics principle "conservation of angular momentum"[5] in action. However, for me, this is an example of just how magical cats really are. It shows a being totally in tune with their bodies and their surroundings, and what could be more magical than that? In fact, it's such an awesome skill that it gave rise to the belief that 'a cat always lands on its feet'. This, in turn, became an idiomatic expression, where describing someone as 'landing on their feet' meant that they had come out of a difficult situation unscathed or having, somehow, benefitted. Here we see the Physical Cat's abilities becoming an affirmation of the Idiomatic Cat.

Another fascinating physical attribute of the cat is their brain, which is a lot more complex than many people realise. If we compare cats with humans' other favourite pet, the dog, we find that their brains are a lot more complex. For example, a cat's cerebral cortex, which is the part of the brain responsible for rational decision making and thought process, has "almost 300 million nerve cells compared to about 160 million in the dog".[6] There is also evidence that "Cats have a longer-term memory than dogs"[7] and can easily recognise and identify their human companions, even after a significant period of absence. Cats also have the capacity to learn through observation and will try to work out how they can emulate what their human is doing. If your cat is watching you open a cupboard, they may well be planning an attempt to get in there when you are not around. As someone who had to change their fridge to stop repeated raids by a pair of skilled and intelligent felines, I feel duty bound to pass on the warning!

A cat's super-intelligent brain is sent information by a series of highly attuned senses. Take their sense of hearing, for example. Cats hear a broader range of sound than most other mammals. In terms of lower-level sounds, cats can hear about the same as most other mammals, including humans. However, it is the higher register of sound where cats have a real advantage. While humans can only hear as high as 20kHz, a "cat can register sounds up to 64kHz, some 1.6 octaves higher than [a human] and a full octave higher than a dog".[8] To put it another way, "At the higher levels, humans in the prime of life can hear noises up to about 20,000 cycles a second. This sinks to around 12,000 cycles per second in humans of retirement age. Dogs can manage up to 35,000 to 40,000 cycles per second, so that they are able to detect sounds that we cannot. Cats, on the other hand, can hear sounds up to an astonishing 100,000 cycles per second".[9] The effectiveness of cats' hearing is augmented by their ability to swivel and rotate their ears independently of each other to help focus on particular sounds. They have 32 muscles controlling their ears, which can also be flattened against their skull if they feel threatened. By flattening their ears in a fight, cats ensure they protect the effectiveness of one of their greatest sensory assets.

Cats also have an incredibly attuned sense of smell. The have a significantly greater number of cell receptors in their noses than humans: "The human nose contains about 5 million olfactory receptors that detect aromas, while a cat's nose has 45 to 80 (possibly up to 200) million scent receptors".[10] This means that a cat's sense of smell is approximately fourteen times more sensitive than that of a human. Their nose is augmented with the cat's Jacobson's organ, which is positioned between the septum of their nose and the hard palate of the mouth. To use this organ, a cat will raise its top lip, almost as if it is sneering or has smelled something nasty. This is called the Flehmen response and is a sign that the cat is drawing in and savouring various aromas. If you see you cat with their head back, gulping in the air, they are probably using their Jacobson's organ to work something out. Cats get and receive much of their information and can communicate through scent, as we shall see later in this chapter.

While your cat may have a profound sense of smell, they really do not have a particularly good sense of taste. Cats only have just under five hundred taste buds on their tongue, meaning that they cannot taste sweet things. By way of comparison, humans tend to have around nine thousand tastebuds so can experience a more varied palate of flavours. Instead, cats' tongues are equipped with "papillae, stiff, hooked, backward-facing spines"[11] which they use to comb their fur. While focusing on the cat's mouth, it's worth noting that cats don't really chew their food, because their teeth are not the right shape to allow them to do so. They tend to rip larger chunks of food and swallow them pretty much whole. Neither can cats pucker their lips to suck, which is why they lap at water.

Of course, when we think about a cat's senses, the most magical of those is their eyesight, those ever changing, moonlike orbs which have led to so much myth and poetry. As we have noted several times, "The muscles in the iris [of a cat's eye] expand and contract to protect the inner eye from sunlight",[12] giving their eyes a changeable quality. Like most other predators, a cat's eyes are positioned on the front of their faces and are "large in comparison to their skull".[13] They have a third eyelid, called a haw or nictitating membrane, which helps to protect and lubricate the surface of their cornea. At the back of their eyes is a feature which helps to intensify the image a cat sees, "a light reflecting layer called the *tapetum lucidum* (meaning literally 'bright carpet'), which acts rather like a mirror behind the retina, reflecting light back to the retinal cells. With this, the cat can utilize every scrap of light that enters its eyes".[14] It is this layer which means that a cat's eyes seem to glow in the dark and which gave Percy Shaw the inspiration to create the small 'cat's eyes' which line many of our roads – another piece of magical cat inspiration being used in the real world. Because of the *tapetum lucidum*, cats only need a sixth of the light that a human needs to be able to see, and they can see in a whole different spectrum: "since the publication of a 2014 study, scientists have come to realise that a significant number of the photons [a cat can see] are floating in the ultraviolet end of the spectrum, which means that cats can see a whole world that is quite invisible to us".[15] Not only can your cat see better than you, but it can also see things that you can't.

However, despite all of this, cats cannot focus their eyes under a distance of 25cm, which is when they rely on their whiskers, or vibrissae, to give them information. These are large tactile hairs which are found in several places on a cat's body. The most obvious are on their cheeks and above their eyes, but they also have them on their chin and the back of their legs. These reinforced hairs are not there to help a cat measure a space to see if it is big enough for them to fit through, although this is what many people believe. Whiskers are, in fact, primarily used to detect changes in air currents. "As the cat moves along in the dark it needs to manoeuvre past solid objects. Each solid object it approaches causes slight eddies in the air, minute disturbances of air movement, and the cat's whiskers are so sensitive that they can read the air changes and respond to the presence of solid obstacles even without touching them".[16] Whiskers are an incredibly sensitive tool which cats also rely on when hunting.

As we have seen, the Physical Cat is a truly magical being, equipped with a complex brain, agile body and heightened senses. Much of what we have discussed so far relates to how their physicality aids the cat when hunting and exploring, but a cat also uses its whole body as a way of communicating. For example, cat's eyes are not just for seeing but for signalling to others how they are feeling. A cat with fully open eyes is alert to what is going on around them. "If the animal switches to half-closed eyes, this is an expression of total relaxation signalling complete trust in the friendship of its owners".[17] In our household, we call this 'friendly eyes', when one of the boys seems to squint or blink at us. This eye movement it is a sign of affection and contentment and is something humans should learn to emulate to communicate with their feline. Cats will also totally close their eyes as a sign of complete submission if they are involved in a confrontation. And it isn't only our cat's eyelids we should be watching. Their pupils will dilate both when they are happy and when they are threatened, in much the same way as they react to light. However, it won't just be their eyes that react if a cat is feeling threatened, as there will normally be another physical response, such as the hairs along their back and tail standing on end.

In fact, humans should really look at their cat's tail as much as their eyes, as cats use it to send more information than we may realise. One position that most people who live with cats will be familiar with is a tail "upright and ramrod straight except for a short length at the tip, which waves around freely like a semaphore flag".[18] This tail position is used by kittens when they see their mother and is a sign of deep affection and trust. If a cat walks towards you with their tail in this position, then you've been adopted as their pseudo-parent.

Another fairly sure sign that a cat has laid claim to you is if they rub against you. "While walking their territory", Grey writes, "They rub themselves on fences, walls, on the grass, paths and even on humans to show that this territory belongs to them".[19] Yes, unfortunately, the cat that greets you with a warm rub past your face when you wake up, or against your leg when they come in from an evening's walk, probably isn't being affectionate but is marking you with their pheromones. Cats have pheromone releasing scent glands on their chin, lips, cheeks, on the pads of their feet and at the base of their tails. They also release pheromones in their urine. These pheromones give other cats an incredible amount of information, telling them not only which cats have been in the area but also when they were last there. Even the way that a cat leaves its faeces can be an indication of ownership or marking of territory. If faeces are left uncovered then the cat is probably laying claim to the territory while if they cover their faeces, it is a sign that the cat does not really want anyone to know that they have been there.

You've probably noticed that there is one significant aspect of cat communication I have so far avoided – nowhere have I mentioned any form of verbal communication. This may seem odd, considering that I finished the last chapter discussing the homophonic similarity between the Egyptian god Mau and the meowing sound that we hear from our cats. However, if you read that section closely you will have noticed that I gave two options for the similarity between those noises. Firstly, that the word 'Mau' was coined after the sound a cat was making and, secondly, that the cat began using the sound because it learned it from humans. That's because adult cats do not communicate verbally with each other, beyond the occasional yowl if they are threatened. "Kittens meow to let their mother know they're cold or hungry, but once they get a bit older, cats no longer meow to other cats".[20] The likely reason why cats began meowing to humans in the past is that we, as a species, are really bad at picking up the messages they send us with their eyes and tails. Cats learned that humans need an audible nudge to really get the hint and so they began meowing at us.

The fact that cats learned to meow at humans is not surprising, given the complexity of their cerebral cortex. There is also some evidence that another noise made by cats has been developed after taking notice of a different species:

It seems likely that the similarity between the hiss of a cat and that of a snake is not accidental. It has been claimed that the feline hiss is a case of protective mimicry. In other words, the cat imitates the snake to give an enemy the impression that it too is venomous and dangerous... Supporting this idea is the fact that cats often add spitting to hissing. Spitting is another way in which threatened snakes react.[21]

What this shows us is that cats are clever, they learn and adapt to different circumstances and it's possible that they may be doing the same now. There are several online videos which appear to show cats communicating with each other, verbally.[22] What's notable about these videos is that, if you play them when your own cats are in the room, they tend to stop and listen to what is being 'said'. So, rather than saying that cats *do not* communicate with each other verbally it may be more accurate to say that, previously, cats *have not* communicated with each other verbally.

After all, many of the aspects of the Physical Cat that appear so magical are simply adaptations to particular environmental and social factors. The Physical Cat is the result of millennia of changes and it is possible that, in the twenty-first century, humans may be accelerating this process. But, to find out exactly how we affecting our beloved felines, we will need to make the leap into the fast-changing world of the Evolving Cat.

Chapter 6

The Cat of the Day – The Evolving Cat

The Evolving Cat by Hannah Willow

Despite a chequered history of humans and cats, and the persistence of the belief that cats are somewhat aloof, they are now the second most popular pet on the planet. The first decades of the twenty-first century have seen cat lovers go online with pictures of their felines and create incredibly popular content on social media. This has become such a popular pastime that it has spawned several cat 'celebrities' and there is even a Wikipedia page devoted to the subject of cats and the internet![1] There have also been changes to the way that we keep cats, with around ten percent now being kept indoors as house cats.[2] These changes in the way we perceive and keep cats is leading to changes in the way cats behave. While some people have concerns about such changes, insisting that cats should be allowed to behave according to their natural instincts, it's worth noting that cats have been adapting and evolving to the needs of humans for thousands of years. This has led to the cat leading something of a double life:

> In the home it is an overgrown kitten gazing up at its human owners. Out on the tiles it is fully adult, its own boss, a free-living wild creature, alert and self-sufficient, its human protector for the moment completely out of mind.[3]

We have already seen that a cat's meow is a remnant of kittenhood which cats don't tend to continue as adults, unless they live with humans. Similarly, cats will pummel or knead their human owners, another action from kittenhood when they kneed their mothers' bellies to stimulate the flow of milk. It's clear that cats don't see humans as their owners but as surrogate parents.

Humans have been embracing their role as pseudo-parents for millennia. For example, you may think that the naming of cats is a recent phenomenon, however, there is some evidence that Egyptians named their felines. The first recorded name of a cat is "Nedjem", dating from around 1400 BCE.[4] It's a surprisingly lovely name, translating from Egyptian as 'sweet' or 'pleasant'. Yes, the first recorded name for a cat is, essentially, 'sweetie', something I call my boys on a daily basis! As noted in an earlier chapter, cats were so beloved by Egyptians that if a cat died, the humans in their household went into a period of mourning. Conversely, we can feel the absolute joy seventeen-year-old Emperor Udo of Japan when he wrote the following about his cat on March 11, 889CE:

> Taking a moment of my free time, I wish to express my joy of the cat. It arrived by boat as a gift to the late Emperor,

received from the hands of Minamoto no Kuwashi. The color of the fur is peerless. None could find the words to describe it, although one said it was reminiscent of the deepest ink. It has an air about it, similar to Kanno. Its length is 5 sun, and its height is 6 sun. I affixed a bow about its neck, but it did not remain for long.

In rebellion, it narrows its eyes and extends its needles. It shows its back.

When it lies down, it curls in a circle like a coin. You cannot see its feet. It's as if it were circular Bi disk. When it stands, its cry expresses profound loneliness, like a black dragon floating above the clouds.

By nature, it likes to stalk birds. It lowers its head and works its tail. It can extend its spine to raise its height by at least 2 sun. Its color allows it to disappear at night. I am convinced it is superior to all other cats.[5]

Udo's reaction is that his cat is the best in the world. Don't we all live we a feline that we think is 'superior to all other cats'?

We see evidence of this adoring relationship between humans and their companion cats around the world. The Prophet Muhammed loved his cat Muezza so much that, rather than disturbing her when she had fallen asleep on his robe, he cut the sleeve off so that she could continue to sleep in peace.[6] Chinese emperor Zhu Houcong erected a tombstone to his beloved feline, Xuemei, when they died.[7] Lexicographer Samuel Johnson famously worshipped his cat, Hodge, a statue of whom now stands outside his London home. Similarly, writer Edward Lear, who composed the charming nonsense poem *The Owl and the Pussy Cat*, clearly adored his cat, Foss, and saw cats as "a symbol of joy and life".[8]

So, where did this relationship between humans and cats, which has had such a profound influence on the development of both species, begin? Well, that's a difficult to answer, as there is evidence which hints that humans and cats were living alongside each other much earlier than we may imagine. Deborah Blake notes that "There is evidence that wildcats first lived among people over 100,000 years ago in Mesopotamia",[9] while John Bradshaw states that "It is likely that the first people to tame wildcats were the Natufians, who inhabited the Levant from about 13,000 to 10,000 years ago".[10] Brennan points to "southern Cyprus where excavations of a 9,500-year-old burial have unearthed to skeletons: one of a human, the other of a cat".[11] However, the first written evidence of some form of domestication of cats is from the Egyptians "whose meticulous record-keeping leaves us with little doubt that there was definitely a developed relationship between cats and humanity in the earliest days of their civilisation".[12]

At this stage, the cat's main role was to help preserve grain stores from being eaten by rodents and other vermin, although we can see from the naming of Nedjem that they weren't simply working animals and were held in high esteem. We soon begin to see the spread of the domesticated cat in the historical record: "There are early (fifth and sixth century BCE) literary references to domesticated cats in Greece and China and a few hundred years later they appear in Sanskrit writings of India. By CE 60, there were domestic cats in Japan and across the Middle East. It took another few hundred years for Felis Catus to reach Britain, but by CE 936 the Welsh prince Howel Dda was enacting legislation for their protection".[13] As cats became domesticated around the world, their role changed and they were no longer simply associated with protecting grain stores. They became symbols of the hearth and home, presumably because they love curling up in front of a warm fire. However, this role became fraught with danger for some of their species:

Cats were therefore thought to be protective animals and were enclosed in walls and floors so that their spirits might protect the home. Cats were walled up alive into buildings as protection.[14]

This was just the beginning of several centuries of persecution, as we have seen, when cats became associated with witchcraft and the Devil.

But how did cats move from a creature feared so much they were ritually sacrificed to one which we welcomed into our homes and onto our laps? Well, in Britain at least it has been suggested that it was the cat's roots in Egypt which began to change attitudes.

There was a lot of archaeological excavation going on in Egypt during the nineteenth century, much of it widely reported in the British newspapers. Readers lapped up exotic stories about the ancient worship of cats and the sacred images of the goddess Bastet.[15]

While this is an entirely plausible reason for cat's return to popularity, it strikes me that there is a more potent one – the decline of superstition and the advance of science. In 1859, Charles Darwin published his revolutionary book *On the Origin of Species*, which showed how populations of animals evolved over time because of the process of natural selection, where favourable traits are maintained while unfavourable ones are eventually bred out over generations. The application of Darwin's theory led to direct changes in cat physiology in the nineteenth century with "competitive cat shows and pedigree cat breeding".[16]

However, it wasn't just that humans were selectively breeding cats during this period; felines had, themselves, been evolving over thousands of years and had "developed a set of personal characteristics that make them all but irresistibly attractive to humans".[17] Traits such as meowing and purring, which cats normally stop after kittenhood, are part of a "set of behaviours humans find entertaining, amusing or just plain adorable".[18] Essentially cats evolved to retain these behaviours into adulthood because they found them beneficial. However, there is also evidence that cats have not only retained but developed behaviour specifically to appeal to humans. A 2009 study entitled *The cry embedded within the purr* found a notable difference between a cat's solicitation and non-solicitation purrs. A non-solicitation purr is the sound that we generally hear from a cat when they sit on our laps and are happy. A solicitation purr is the sound a cat makes when they want something, and it is generally louder and faster. The study found that the frequency of the solicitation purr is higher and makes humans feel a greater sense of compulsion to respond to the needs of the cat. The study noted that the frequency of the solicitation purr was the same as the cry of a human child in distress, suggesting that "the purr could serve as a subtle means of exploitation"[19] by the cat. That's right; cats have evolved a specific sound that makes you much more likely to do as they wish!

While that makes it sound as though cats are having it all their own way, humans get an awful lot from our relationship with cats. It is a symbiotic relation, one where the close proximity of two organisms leads to mutual benefits. Modern forms of pest control and higher standards in sanitation means that we no longer need cats to keep rats and mice away from our food supplies and yet we still keep them in our homes. They have come to fulfil a very different function in our lives:

> The relationship between human and cat is touching in both senses of the word. The cat rubs against its owner's body and the owner strokes and fondles the cat's fur. If such owners are wired up in the laboratory to test their physiological responses, it is found that their body systems become markedly calmer when they start stroking their cats.[20]

This is because "stroking a cat produces a cloud of negative ions"[21] which makes humans feel happy and relaxed. Humans also form a "psychological relationship [with cats] which lacks the complexities, betrayals and contradictions of human relationships",[22] meaning that we tend to find our relationship with cats feels unconditional and, therefore, more fulfilling. All of this has profound benefits for humans:

> a special study in the United States has recently revealed that, for those whose stress has led to heart trouble, the owning of a cat may literally make the difference between life and death, reducing blood pressure and calming the overworked heart.[23]

To find one of our cats real healing superpowers, we have to return to their purring. We have already seen how they have adapted their solicitation purr specifically to appeal to us, but it is their non-solicitation purr which is really magical. Again, it is another vocal trait left over from kittenhood, where kittens will either purr or meow to let their mothers know that they are hungry. In adulthood it is usually a sign of contentment, although cats will also purr when they are feeling unwell. This is because purring has significant therapeutic qualities for the cat and for the human they are sitting on. "Cats purr at frequencies between 25 and 50 Hz with extensions up to 1540 Hz. Experimental research has shown that the 25 to 50 Hz range of frequencies promotes bone strength by 20 per cent and not only stimulates the healing of fractures but also the speed at which healing takes place".[24] It is not just bones that a cat's purr can heal:

> Sound vibrations between 50 and 150 Hz administered at low volume have been found to relieve both acute and chronic pain ... [while] Vibrational applications in the 20 to 140 Hz range has proven effective in reducing swelling, healing

wounds, repairing damaged muscle and tendon, increasing joint mobility and even easing shortness of breath.[25]

This is the magic of the Evolving Cat; a simple sound, maintained from kittenhood and used in their social interaction with humans, which has a profoundly therapeutic effect on our bodies.

Of course, humanity's relationship with cat is not without its issues, the most pressing of which is the impact cats have on the wildlife around their homes. Cats may play the role of a kitten when with humans but they have a reputation as fearsome hunters and some of them tend to bring home dead – or partially dead – prey. There could be a couple of reasons why they do this. The first is that cats have a territory which belongs to them. If they catch their prey elsewhere, it makes sense that they would bring their prey back to their own territory, where they feel safest, to eat it. However, this doesn't explain why some cats seem to present their prey to their humans. What we witness here is a bit of role reversal: "Although usually they look upon humans as pseudo parents, on these occasions they view them as their family – in other words, their kittens".[26] When your cat brings home prey, it is trying to get you to kill and eat the prey. The cat is responding to a natural urge to pass on its skills to its family, which explains why it is unneutered female cats who are most likely to exhibit this behaviour. While it may be a nice thing for the cat to do (and you are encouraged to praise rather than scold your cat when they bring home such 'treat') it's not always a great thing to have to deal with, particularly if you have to find and somehow trap a wounded and panicked small mammal which is running around your home.

It is the cumulative effect that this behaviour has on biodiversity which is of most concern. In a suburban area with a significant number of domestic cats, the impact could be considerable. A recent international study into the effect of felines on biodiversity found that cats had been implicated "in the global extinction of at least 63 species — 40 birds, 21 mammals, two reptiles"[27] while a heart-breaking news story in 2021 revealed that "A record-breaking bat that flew more than 1,200 miles (2,018 km) from London to Russia died after being attacked by a cat".[28] Cats do have a significant impact on other creatures that live around them, not only through predation but also through fear. The mere presence or scent of a cat can "influence foraging and defence behaviours, stress responses, energy income and body condition, vulnerability to other predators, and reproductive investment and output"[29] in a range of local wildlife. This has led to calls for "the total removal of feral and other unowned cats"[30] so that nature can recover.

This call is not universal, however, with others noting that the type of prey killed by cats is significant: "Evidence suggests that cat predation is often 'compensatory predation' — preying on animals that would likely have died anyway from disease or hunger. Studies show that the animals caught by predators are generally weaker and more diseased than those killed by manmade sources".[31] In this sense, domestic cats could be seen as aiding the process of natural selection, helping a range of prey species to evolve and adapt to their presence.

However, there is also a sense that cats' hunting behaviour is beginning to change and the main factor behind this change is their relationship with humans. In 2013, BBC television reported a study on the behaviour of domestic cats, led by Dr John Bradshaw from the University of Bristol and Dr Sarah Ellis from the University of Lincoln. Called *The Secret Life of Cats*, the study took place in the village of Shamley Green, Surrey, where fifty cats were monitored over a week. The study revealed a number of surprising behavioural changes in cats as they adapted to the needs of their human influenced environment. One of the key findings was that the cats in the village were not hunting as much as expected. While the researchers considered that bad weather during the week of the experiment may have had an effect on their results, they found a more surprising reason for the change. Instead of hunting, the cats were going into each other's homes and eating the food which had been put down by humans. The researchers concluded that the cats were getting enough nutrition from the food they were given and didn't need to hunt. This finding directly challenged the view of cats as indiscriminate killing machines and suggested that their behaviour was evolving because they lived with humans.

The programme also reported other surprising changes in cat behaviour. The research team found that there were significantly fewer territorial fights between the cats than they were expecting. With fifty felines in such a small space, they reported that cats were able to share territory with each other peacefully. They followed two felines called Phoebe and Kato from neighbouring houses and found that they both used the same territory, but not at the same time. When Kato went out, Phoebe stayed home and vice versa. The research team found the same behaviour happening all over the village. Perhaps even more surprisingly, they found one household of six unrelated cats living together and getting on well. Our previous understanding suggested that domestic cats were solitary animals and would not tolerate living in a large group, and yet here was a group of cats not only tolerating each other but congregating in the same territorial space at the same time and even grooming each other.

The research concluded that cats were evolving quickly because humans wanted and needed them to. Much of the wild behaviour cats exhibit was dropping away and they were keeping more of their juvenile characteristics. Early on in this chapter, I quoted Desmond Morris' assertion that "In the home [the cat] is an overgrown kitten gazing up at its human owners. Out on the tiles it is fully adult, its own boss, a free-living wild creature, alert and self-sufficient, its human protector for the moment completely out of mind".[32] It is entirely possible that this is no longer the case for many cats.

The next question we need to ask ourselves is how we feel

about these changes. Do we accept that the relationship between cats and humans is changing the nature of our felines, or do we cling to the idea that our cats need to be, at least partially, wild?

I can only speak for myself here but, personally, I embrace these changes. Probably the most significant motivator for me to write this book was that there were significant aspects of my cats' behaviour I could not align with the archetypes explored in other texts about cats and magic. I found them far more social, less mysterious and aloof than the felines presented in those books. It may very well be true that humans are making cats retain more and more of their kitten aspects, which some see as us stunting their natural development. However, what we have seen is that cats have already retained a number of juvenile behaviours, such as meowing, purring and pummelling, during their long association with humans. The modern domestic cat does not have the same life as the vermin catchers of ancient Egypt, nor even the witch's cat of the Medieval period. The process of domestication is an evolution and cats continue to respond to that, to strengthen the symbiotic bond we have between us. To dismiss this and continue harking back to what we think a cat should be is to deny the true magic of cats.

The Evolving Cat is changing quickly and will continue to do so, augmenting the Physical Cat with more magical traits and abilities. Standing firmly in the physical world, they help their human partners to create versions of the Idiomatic Cat, so that we can express how we feel about the world around us. These three aspects of the Cat of the Day give us a fresh perspective on the magic of cats. In terms of both our relationship and our understanding with the Cat of the Day, it's as if we are standing in the first golden rays of dawn.

Of course, our cats are a mix of the qualities of both the Cats of the Night and the Day. The new, emerging archetype does not simply wash away the old. Cats still sit among the stars yet they can also stand, rooted, upon the Earth. These beautiful, magical companion animals have lit up our history, revealed humanity at its worst and shown us how to love unconditionally. Our relationship with them has been one of change, of waxing and waning, of darkness and light, of the night and the day. That is the real magic of cats.

Appendix

The Cat of the Night and the Cat of the Day
(a story for kittens of all ages)

The Cat of the Night and the Cat of the Day by Hannah Willow

Below is the original version of my poem, *The Cat of the Night and the Cat of the Day*, which inspired the structure of this book. The poem imagines a story told by a mother cat to her kittens, explaining how the world was created and why we alternate between periods of light and dark. I hope you enjoy it!

Long, long ago, before there was time,
Before there was music, or stories, or rhyme,
The Moon loved the Sun so much she gave birth
to small little planet, which we call the Earth.

The Moon loved the Earth, with its rivers and seas,
The Sun loved the Earth, with its mountains and trees;
Each wanted to give their new child a toy
To show the Earth how she had filled them with joy.

Moon spoke to the Stars for help with the task.
"What gift can I give?" she started to ask,
When, out of her skirt, giving her such a fright,
Rolled a little black cat called The Cat of the Night.

The Cat of the Night was a black, black cat,
A cat so black he was blacker than black;
So black that underneath his coat
Was every other colour, dancing.

And Moon so loved the Cat of the Night
She bathed his heart in purest light.
The stars drew close to see him blessed
With a white, white moon on his black, black chest.

The little back cat twitched his little black nose
As the Stars lay a kiss on his little black toes.
He skipped as they tickled, he jumped left and right
When each of his paws turned bright, brilliant white.

So, the Cat of the Night with the black, black nose,
With the moon on his chest and stars on his toes,
Was a gift to the Earth, as a sign of great love,
From her Silvery Mother in the dark sky above.

Sun ran to his friends, the Clouds, in such fright:
"Oh, Clouds, have you seen the Cat of the Night?
I need a good gift" he started to say
When out of his crown rolled the Cat of the Day.

The Cat of the Day was a white, white cat
A cat so white, he was whiter than white,
So white that underneath his coat
Was every other colour, dancing.

And Sun so loved the Cat of the Day
He chased his friends, the Clouds, away,
Then filled the cat's belly with deep golden heat
Which coloured his tail, his body and feet.

The Clouds gathered round where the golden cat laid
And crisscrossed his back with a deep, cooling shade.
He lolled and he wriggled, he stretched and he rolled
As his coat became striped with a deepening gold.

So, the Cat of the Day with the pink, pink nose,
With a dark stripey back and bright golden toes,
Was a gift to the Earth, as a sign of great love,
From her Firey Father in the bright sky above.

The Earth loved the Moon and the Earth loved the Sun
And Earth loved the cats and would cuddle each one.
When the cats saw each other they wanted to play,
And started a race which goes on to this day.

They race and they chase, and they chase and they run
Because running and racing and chasing is fun.
They chase from the East and they race to the West
Because running and racing and chasing is best.

Each morning, at sunrise, the Cat of the Day
Rolls over the hills chasing night time away.
At sunset the other one rolls into sight,
And darkness belongs to the Cat of the Night.

In Summer the daytimes are longer and bright
When the Cat of the Day beats the Cat of the Night;
In Winter the Cat of the Night wins the sport,
So, night times are long and day times are short.

They chase from the East and they race to the West
Because running and racing and chasing is best.
They race and they chase, and they chase and they run
Because running and racing and chasing is fun.

Moon follows the Night, Sun follows the Day
As they run and they race and they chase and they play.
Each follows the cat they created from love
Looking down on the game from the skies up above.

Earth still loves the Moon, Earth still loves the Sun,
Earth still loves the cats and embraces each one.
And the chase still goes on, because that's how they play:
The Cat of the Night and the Cat of the Day.

Endnotes

Introduction
1.   Gettings (1989) p1

Chapter 1: The Cat of the Night – The Universal Cat
1.   Gettings (1989) p102
2.   Blake (2010) p59
3.   Franklin (1997) p86
4.   Gettings (1989) p1
5.   Yeats (2008) p141
6.   Yeats (2008) p141
7.   Franklin (1997) p86
8.   Carroll (2009) p59
9.   Gray (2012) p26
10.   Pang (2018) p57
11.   Blake (2018) p9
12.   Morris (1992) p9
13.   Gray (2012) p35
14.   Brennan (2017) p121
15.   Brennan (2017) p120
16.   Gray (2012) p35
17.   Gray (2012) p38
18.   Gray (2012) p38
19.   https://egyptianmuseum.org/deities-sekhmet (accessed 20.12.2021)
20.   Gray (2012) p39
21.   Gray (2012) p52
22.   Franklin (1997) p88
23.   Gettings (1989) p47
24.   Crossley-Holland (2011) pxxx
25.   Ellis Davidson (1990) p120

Chapter 2: The Cat of the Night – The Witch's Cat

1. Morris (1992) p212
2. Morris (1992) p10
3. Moray Williams (1942) p3
4. Moray Williams (1942) p206
5. Masefield (1927) p101
6. Gray (2012) p44
7. Gettings (1989) pp36-37
8. Gray (2012) p44
9. Gettings (1989) p178
10. Gettings (1898) p168
11. Gettings (1989) p37
12. Gettings (1989) p170
13. www.collinsdictionary.com/dictionary/english/brindled (accessed 23.12.21)
14. Moray Williams (1942) p5
15. www.thehappycatsite.com/brindle-cat/ (accessed 23.12.2021)
16. Blake (2018) p33
17. Brennan (2017) pxii
18. Gray (2012) pp44-45
19. Morris (1992) p210
20. Morris (1992) p210
21. Morris (1992) p211
22. Franklin (1997) p89
23. Gray (2012) p45
24. Gettings (1989) p180
25. Franklin (1997) p89
26. www.historyextra.com/period/medieval/black-death-plague-epidemic-facts-what-caused-rats-fleas-how-many-died/ (accessed 27.12.2012)
27. Brennan (2017) p143

Chapter 3: The Cat of the Night – The Knowing Cat

1. Dale-Green, Patricia, *The Cult of the Cat*, quoted in Gettings

(1989) p1

2. Gettings (1989) p152
3. Grey (2012) p24
4. Parker (2001) p70
5. Gettings (1989) pp80-81
6. Gettings (1989) p82
7. Gettings (1989) p74
8. Gettings (1989) p80
9. Brennan (2017) p186
10. Brennan (2017) p188
11. Gettings (1989) p1
12. Carr-Gomm, (2019) p54
13. Gettings (1989) p18
14. Grey (2012) p24
15. Morris (1992) p162
16. reported in Gettings (1989) pp83-84
17. Brennan (2017) p62
18. https://thehill.com/changing-america/enrichment/arts-culture/581162-new-study-shows-how-cats-track-their-owners (accessed 28.12.2021)
19. Quoted in Brennan (2017) p71
20. Gettings (1989) p86
21. Reported in Gettings (1989) pp85-86
22. Brennan (2017) p132
23. Carr-Gomm (2019) p57
24. https://www.poetryfoundation.org/poetrymagazine/browse?contentId=35341 (accessed 28.12.2021)

Who is The Cat of the Day?

1. Grey (2012) p24
2. Morris (1992) p1

Chapter 4: The Cat of the Day – The Idiomatic Cat

1. Brennan (2017) p126

2. Carter (2008) p15
3. Westwood and Simpson (2006) p473
4. Westwood and Simpson (2006) p473
5. Gettings (1989) p59
6. Westwood and Simpson (2006) p474
7. Told by Brennan (2017) pp128-129
8. https://www.tokyo-smart.com/en/blog/news/maneki-neko (accessed 30.12.2021)
9. Carroll (2009) p76
10. quoted at https://wordhistories.net/2016/12/15/cat-may-look-at-king/ (accessed 30.12.2021)
11. https://wordhistories.net/2016/12/15/cat-may-look-at-king/ (accessed 30.12.2021)
12. Morris (1992) p217
13. Morris (1992) p163
14. https://www.phrases.org.uk/meanings/let-the-cat-out-of-the-bag.html (accessed 30.12.2021)
15. quoted at https://wordhistories.net/2016/12/04/not-a-cat-in-hells-chance/ (accessed 30.12.2021)
16. quoted at https://wordhistories.net/2016/12/04/not-a-cat-in-hells-chance/ (accessed 30.12.2021)
17. Morris (1992) p227
18. Morris (1992) p227
19. Franklin (1997) p94
20. Gettings (1998) p186
21. https://www.phrases.org.uk/meanings/curiosity-killed-the-cat.html (accessed 30.12.2021)
22. https://wordhistories.net/2017/03/19/the-cats-whiskers/ (accessed 30.12.2021)
23. Morris (1992) p220
24. Gettings (1998) p34
25. https://wamiz.co.uk/cat/breeds/496/egyptian-mau (accessed 30.12.2021)

Chapter 5: The Cat of the Day – The Physical Cat

1. Gray (2012) p3
2. Brennan (2017) p114
3. Brennan (2017) p18
4. Morris (1992) p30
5. https://www.real-world-physics-problems.com/Real_World_Physics_Problems_Newsletter-cat-righting-reflex.htmlc (accessed 31.12.2021)
6. https://www.catster.com/lifestyle/cat-facts-anatomy-your-cats-brain (accessed 31.12.2021)
7. Blake (2018) p20
8. Brennan (2017) p83
9. Morris (1992) p19
10. https://vcahospitals.com/know-your-pet/why-cats-sniff-butts (accessed 31.12.2021)
11. Brennan (2017) p12
12. Grey (2012) p25
13. Grey (2012) p25
14. Morris (1992) p33
15. Brennan (2017) p82
16. Morris (1992) p31
17. Morris (1992) p37
18. Brennan (2017) p35
19. Grey (2012) p26
20. https://www.aspca.org/pet-care/cat-care/common-cat-behavior-issues/meowing-and-yowling (accessed 31.12.2021)
21. Morris (1992) p108
22. a notable example can be found at: https://www.youtube.com/watch?v=z3U0udLH974 (accessed 31.12.2021)

Chapter 6: The Cat of the Day – The Evolving Cat

1. https://en.wikipedia.org/wiki/Cats_and_the_Internet (accessed 02.01.2022)
2. https://www.bluecross.org.uk/pet-advice/indoor-cats

(accessed 02.01.2022)

3. Morris (1992) p1
4. https://www.guinnessworldrecords.com/world-records/
   first-named-cat (accessed 02.01.2022)
5. https://shirleytwofeathers.com/The_Blog/itsacatastrophe/
   category/historical-cats/ (accessed 02.01.2022)
6. https://theislamicinformation.com/blogs/prophet-
   muhammad-pbuh-muezza-favorite-cat/ (accessed 02.01.2022)
7 https://www.chinawhisper.com/the-10-chinese-emperors-
   with-strange-quirks (accessed 02.01.2022)
8. Gettings (1989) p61
9. Blake (2018) p8
10. https://www.washingtonpost.com/national/health-science/
    dogs-we-understand-cats-are-mysterious-even-though-
    they-are-the-most-popular-pet/2013/10/14/2c59c6b0-26ca-
    11e3-ad0d-b7c8d2a594b9_story.html (accessed 02.01.2022)
11. Brennan (2017) p114
12. Brennan (2017) pp114-115
13. Brennan (2017) p124
14. Franklin (1997) p86
15. Brennan (2017) p144
16. Morris (1992) p11
17. Brennan (2017) p218
18. Brennan (2017) p219
19. https://doi.org/10.1016/j.cub.2009.05.033 (accessed 2.1.2022)
20. Morris (1992) p203
21. Brennan (2017) p220
22. Morris (1992) p203
23. Morris (1992) p203
24. Brennan (2017) p221
25. Brennan (2017) pp221-222
26. Morris (1992) p78
27. https://doi.org/10.1002/pan3.10073 (accessed 3.1.2022)
28. https://www.bbc.co.uk/news/uk-58128773 (accessed 3.1.2022)

29. https://doi.org/10.1002/pan3.10073 (accessed 3.1.2022)
30. https://doi.org/10.1002/pan3.10073 (accessed 3.1.2022)
31. https://www.alleycat.org/resources/biology-and-behavior-of-the-cat/ (accessed 3.1.2022)
32. Morris (1992) p1

Bibliography

Blake, William, *Poems selected by James Fenton*, Faber and Faber, London, 2010

Blake, Deborah, *The Little Book of Cat Magic*, Llewellyn Publications, Woodbury, 2018

Brennan, Herbie, *The Mysterious World of Cats*, Coronet, London, 2017

Carr-Gomm, Philip and Stephanie, *The Druid Animal Oracle*, Eddison Books, London, 1996, new edition 2019

Carroll, Lewis, *Alice's Adventures in Wonderland and Through the Looking Glass*, Oxford University Press, Oxford, 2009

Carter, Angela, *The Fairy Tales of Charles Perrault*, Penguin, London, 1977 (2008 edition)

Crossley-Holland, Kevin, *The Penguin Book of Norse Myths*, Penguin, London, 2011

Ellis Davidson, H.R., *Gods and Myths of Northern Europe*, Penguin, London, 1990 (reprinted from 1964)

Franklin, Anna, *Familiars*, Capall Bann Publishing, Chieveley, 1997

Gettings, Fred, *The Secret Lore of Cats*, Grafton Books, London, 1989

Gray, Martha, *Grimalkin: The Witch's Cat*, Moon Books, Winchester, 2012

McComb, Karen et al, *The cry embedded within the purr*, https://doi.org/10.1016/j.cub.2009.05.033 (accessed 2.1.2022)

McCormack, Phillipa and Elvira Martinez Camacho, *Domestic Cats and their impacts on biodiversity: A blindspot in the application of nature conservation law*, https://doi.org/10.1002/pan3.10073 (accessed 3.1.2022)

Morris, Desmond, *Catwatching*, second edition, Arrow Books, London, 1992

Nicoll, Helen, *Meg and Mog*, revised edition, Puffin, London, 2004

Parker, Jessica Dawn, *Animal Wisdom*, Thorsons, London, 2001

Pang, Hannah, *The Moon*, 360 Degrees, London, 2018

Rowling, J.K., *Harry Potter and the Philosopher's Stone*, Bloomsbury, London, 1997

Shakespeare, William, *The Complete Works*, edited by Stanley Wells et al, Oxford University Press, Oxford, 1988

Westwood, Jennifer and Simpson, Jacqueline, *The Lore of the Land*, Penguin, London, 2006

Williams, Ursula Moray, *Gobbolino the Witch's Cat*, Puffin, London, 1942, reissued 2014

Yeats, W.B, *The Collected Poems of W.B. Yeats*, Wordsworth Editions Ltd, Ware, 2008

Media Resources

Hocus Pocus. Dir. Kenny Ortega. Walt Disney Home Video, 2001. DVD

Sabrina the Teenage Witch. Paramount Home Entertainment, 2012. DVD

The Secret Life of Cats, Dir. Helen Sage. BBC, 2013 found at: https://www.dailymotion.com/video/x10w49m

The Uncanny. Dir. Denis Héroux, Network, 2006. DVD

Web pages

www.alleycat.org (accessed 03.01.2022)

www.aspca.org (accessed 31.12.2021)

www.bbc.co.uk/news (accessed 03.01.2022)

www.bluecross.org.uk (accessed 02.01.2022)

www.britannica.com/topic/Lilith-Jewish-folklore (accessed 21.12.2021)

http://www.catsguru.com (accessed 31.12.2021)

www.catster.com (accessed 30.12.2021)

www.chinawhisper.com (accessed 02.01.2022)

www.collinsdictionary.com (accessed 23.12.2021)

https://egyptianmuseum.org/deities-Bastet (accessed 20.12.2021) https://egyptianmuseum.org/deities-sekhmet (accessed 20.12.2021)

www.thehappycatsite.com (accessed 23.12.2021)

www.thehill.com (accessed 28.12.2021)

www.historyextra.com (accessed 27.12.2021)

https://www.iau.org/public/themes/naming_stars/ (accessed 08.12.21)

https://kittehkats.tumblr.com/post/100115334571/the-wonderful-myth-of-chinese-cat-goddess-li-shou (accessed 16.12.21)

www.landofpyramids.org (accessed 29.12.2021)

www.nomnomnow.com (accessed 31.12.2021)

www.phrases.org.uk (accessed 30.12.2021)

www.poetryfoundation.org (accessed 28.12.2021)

www.phrases.org.uk (accessed 30.12.2021)

www.real-world-physics-problems.com (accessed 31.12.2021).

https://shirleytwofeathers.com (accessed 02.01.2022)

https://theislamicinformation.com (accessed 02.01.2022)

www.tokyo-smart.com (accessed 30.12.2021)

https://www.universeguide.com/star/48615/felis (accessed 08.12.21)

https://vcahospitals.com (accessed 31.12.2021)

www.washingtonpost.com (accessed 02.01.2022)

https://wamiz.co.uk (accessed 30.12.2021)

https://en.wikipedia.org/wiki/Cats_and_the_Internet (accessed 02.01.2022)

https://wordhistories.net (accessed 30.12.2021)

www.youtube.com (accessed 31.12.2021)

MOON
BOOKS

PAGANISM & SHAMANISM

What is Paganism? A religion, a spirituality, an alternative belief system, nature worship? You can find support for all these definitions (and many more) in dictionaries, encyclopaedias, and text books of religion, but subscribe to any one and the truth will evade you. Above all Paganism is a creative pursuit, an encounter with reality, an exploration of meaning and an expression of the soul. Druids, Heathens, Wiccans and others, all contribute their insights and literary riches to the Pagan tradition. Moon Books invites you to begin or to deepen your own encounter, right here, right now.

If you have enjoyed this book, why not tell other readers by posting a review on your preferred book site.

Recent bestsellers from Moon Books are:

Journey to the Dark Goddess
How to Return to Your Soul
Jane Meredith
Discover the powerful secrets of the Dark Goddess and
transform your depression, grief and pain into healing
and integration.
Paperback: 978-1-84694-677-6 ebook: 978-1-78099-223-5

Shamanic Reiki
Expanded Ways of Working with Universal Life Force Energy
Llyn Roberts, Robert Levy
Shamanism and Reiki are each powerful ways of healing; together,
their power multiplies. *Shamanic Reiki* introduces techniques to
help healers and Reiki practitioners tap ancient healing wisdom.
Paperback: 978-1-84694-037-8 ebook: 978-1-84694-650-9

Pagan Portals – The Awen Alone
Walking the Path of the Solitary Druid
Joanna van der Hoeven
An introductory guide for the solitary Druid, *The Awen Alone* will
accompany you as you explore, and seek out your own place
within the natural world.
Paperback: 978-1-78279-547-6 ebook: 978-1-78279-546-9

A Kitchen Witch's World of Magical Herbs & Plants
Rachel Patterson
A journey into the magical world of herbs and plants, filled with
magical uses, folklore, history and practical magic. By popular
writer, blogger and kitchen witch, Tansy Firedragon.
Paperback: 978-1-78279-621-3 ebook: 978-1-78279-620-6

Medicine for the Soul
The Complete Book of Shamanic Healing
Ross Heaven
All you will ever need to know about shamanic healing and how to
become your own shaman...
Paperback: 978-1-78099-419-2 ebook: 978-1-78099-420-8

Shaman Pathways – The Druid Shaman
Exploring the Celtic Otherworld
Danu Forest
A practical guide to Celtic shamanism with exercises and
techniques as well as traditional lore for exploring the Celtic
Otherworld.
Paperback: 978-1-78099-615-8 ebook: 978-1-78099-616-5

Traditional Witchcraft for the Woods and Forests
A Witch's Guide to the Woodland with Guided Meditations and
Pathworking
Mélusine Draco
A Witch's guide to walking alone in the woods, with guided
meditations and pathworking.
Paperback: 978-1-84694-803-9 ebook: 978-1-84694-804-6

Wild Earth, Wild Soul
A Manual for an Ecstatic Culture
Bill Pfeiffer
Imagine a nature-based culture so alive and so connected,
spreading like wildfire. This book is the first flame...
Paperback: 978-1-78099-187-0 ebook: 978-1-78099-188-7